FRAMING FLOORS, WALLS, AND CEILINGS

FROM THE EDITORS OF **Fine Homebuilding**®

The Taunton Press

The Taunton Press
Inspiration for hands-on living®

The Taunton Press, Inc., 63 South Main Street, PO Box 5506, Newtown, CT 06470-5506
e-mail: tp@taunton.com

Jacket/Cover design: Cathy Cassidy
Interior design: Cathy Cassidy
Layout: Cathy Cassidy
Front Cover Photographer: Larry Hammerness, courtesy *Fine Homebuilding,* © The Taunton Press, Inc.
Back Cover Photographers: (clockwise from top left) Charles Bickford, courtesy *Fine Homebuilding,*
© The Taunton Press, Inc.; Tom O'Brien, courtesy *Fine Homebuilding,* © The Taunton Press, Inc.;
Roe Osborn, courtesy *Fine Homebuilding,* © The Taunton Press, Inc.; Charles Bickford, courtesy
Fine Homebuilding, © The Taunton Press, Inc.

Taunton's For Pros By Pros® and Fine Homebuilding® are trademarks of
The Taunton Press, Inc., registered in the U.S. Patent and Trademark Office.

Library of Congress Cataloging-in-Publication Data

Framing floors, walls, and ceilings / from the editors of Fine homebuilding.
       p. cm. -- (Taunton's for pros by pros)
   Includes index.
   ISBN 1-56158-758-3
   1. House framing. I. Fine homebuilding. II. For pros, by pros.
   TH2301.F744 2005
   694'.2--dc22

                            2004030090

Printed in the United States of America
10 9 8 7 6 5 4 3 2 1

The following manufacturers/names appearing in *Framing Floors, Walls, and Ceilings* are trademarks:
3M®, Band-Aids®, Blow-In Blanket® System, Bosch®, Construction Master II®, Fortifiber Building Products Systems®,
Linear Link®, Makita®, Milwaukee®, North American Plywood®, Porter-Cable®, Prazi Beam Cutter™, Rust-oleum®,
Simpson®, Simpson Strong Tie®, Sokkia®, Superior Wood Systems®, TrusJoist®, Truss Plate Institute®, Vise-Grip®

Special thanks to the authors, editors, art directors,

copy editors, and other staff members of *Fine Homebuilding*

who contributed to the development of the articles in this book.

CONTENTS

PART 3: FRAMING WALLS

INTRODUCTION

I recently helped a friend remodel the bathroom in his 150-year-old house. The room had been gutted, and the exposed framing was a graphic reminder that we really don't build houses like we used to. The exterior wall was framed with timbers bigger than my leg, and the wall separating the bath from the bedroom was framed with 8-in.-wide chestnut planks. These 1-in.-thick studs were turned flat to provide a broad nailing base for the accordion lath that held the plaster. It was beautiful, at least to a couple of old carpenters, and we wondered for a moment how we might leave it all exposed.

The transition from building with planks and timbers to the way we build houses today started 200 years ago with the invention of a nail-making machine. Methods and materials have evolved continuously over the years. Balloon framing, where the studs ran uninterrupted from foundation to roof, gave way to the platform framing we use today. Studs got smaller. Plywood replaced board sheathing. Nail guns overtook hammers. And so on.

Efforts to make better use of our dwindling forests, to build houses faster, and to make them safer in the wake of hurricanes, earthquakes, and fires have all led to changes in the way we stitch our homes together. If you're building today, you need to keep up with new materials and changing codes. The articles in this book will help you do that (among other things). Collected from past issues of *Fine Homebuilding* magazine, these articles were written by experienced builders. If they lived next door, you'd ask their advice about the header over your new picture window. But good builders aren't that easy to find, which is why we got these folks to write down what they've learned.

—Kevin Ireton
editor-in-chief, *Fine Homebuilding*

All about Headers

■ BY CLAYTON DEKORNE

Like many carpenters in the Northeast, I was taught to frame window and door headers by creating a plywood-and-lumber sandwich, held together with generous globs of construction adhesive and the tight rows of nails that only a nail gun could deliver. Years later, I learned my energetic efforts to build a better header were an exceptional waste of time and resources. Neither the plywood nor the adhesive contributed much strength, only thickness, and this perfect thickness helped only to conduct heat out of the walls during the severe winters common to the region.

At the same time I was laying up lumber sandwiches, young production framers on the West Coast were framing headers efficiently using single-piece 4x12s. They needed only to be chopped to length and filled the wall space above openings, eliminating the need for maddeningly short cripple studs between the top of the header and the wall plate. Nowadays, however, such massive materials are relatively scarce and remarkably expensive, even on the West Coast. So although solid-stock headers certainly save labor, they no longer provide an economical alternative.

With these experiences in mind, I set out to discover some practical alternatives, sur-veying a number of expert framers in different regions of the country. Header framing varies widely from builder to builder and from region to region. Even when factors such as wall thickness and load conditions are made equal, building traditions and individual preferences make for a wide range of header configurations. The examples shown here are just a few of the options possible when you mix and match features, notch cripple studs, and sift in engineered materials. But they aptly demonstrate a number of practical considerations that must be kept in mind when framing a good header.

Big Headers Need More Studs

A header transfers loads from the roof and floors above to the foundation below by way of jack studs (see the drawing on p. 6). This means the header not only must be deep enough (depth refers to the height of a beam: 2x10s are deeper than 2x6s) for a given span to resist bending under load, but also must be supported by jack studs on each end that are part of a load path that continues to the foundation.

The header you choose affects not just strength, but also cost, energy efficiency, and drywall cracking.

Like a Bridge over a Ravine, a Header Spans a Window or Door

Headers are short beams that typically carry roof and floor loads to the sides of openings for doors or windows. Jack studs take over from there, carrying the load to the framing below and eventually to the foundation. That's called the load path, and it must be continuous. The International Residential Code (IRC, the most common code nationwide) has a lot to say about headers, including the tables you need to determine the size header required for most situations. If it's not in the IRC, you need an engineer.

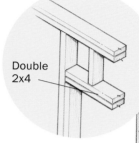

Double 2x4

WHERE YOU DON'T NEED A STRUCTURAL HEADER

In a gable-end wall that doesn't support a load-bearing ridge, or in an interior nonbearing partition, headers up to 8 ft. in length can be built with the same material as the wall studs. Inside, a single 2x is often sufficient, although a double 2x is helpful for securing wide trim. In a gable-end wall, however, a double 2x is needed to help resist the bending loads exerted by the wind.

Load path must be continuous from roof to foundation.

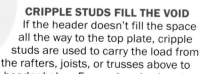

Cripple stud

CRIPPLE STUDS FILL THE VOID

If the header doesn't fill the space all the way to the top plate, cripple studs are used to carry the load from the rafters, joists, or trusses above to the header below. For nonbearing headers, the IRC requires no cripples if the distance to the top plate is less than 24 in.

HIDDEN HEADER

Double rim joist as header

Here's a wood-saving trick. By simply adding an additional member to it, the rim joist above an opening can serve as a header. Two caveats: You'll need to use joist hangers to transfer the load to the header. And if a standard header of this size requires double jack studs, so does a double rim joist.

KINGS HIGH, JACKS LOW

King stud

Header

Jack stud

King studs are the same height as the wall studs, running plate to plate. Nails driven through them into the header's end grain stabilize the header. Jack studs are shorter and fit below the header to carry loads downward. Because longer-spanning headers usually carry greater loads, you may need an extra jack under both ends of big headers. Check your building code.

Installation Guidelines

Typically, header height is established by the door height, and window headers are set at this same height. In homes having 8-ft. ceilings, a header composed of 2x12s or of 2x10s with a flat 2x4 or 2x6 nailer on the bottom accommodates standard 6-ft. 8-in. doors, as shown in the drawing at right.

In a custom home with cathedral ceilings and tall walls, however, header heights can vary widely. And if the doors are a nonstandard height, you'll need to figure out the header height. Finding the height of the bottom of the headers above the subfloor is a matter of adding up the door height, the thickness of the finished-floor materials, and 2½ in. (to allow space for the head jamb and airspace below the door). There are exceptions. Pocket doors typically require a rough opening at least 2 in. higher than a standard door. Windows may include arches or transoms, which affect the rough opening's height.

To find the header length for windows, add 3 in. to the manufacturer's rough-opening dimension if there is to be one jack stud on each side, or 6 in. if two jacks are called for. For doors with single jack studs, add 5½ in. to the door width to allow for jack studs, door jambs, and shim space. If double jacks are needed, then the header should be 8½ in. longer than the door width.

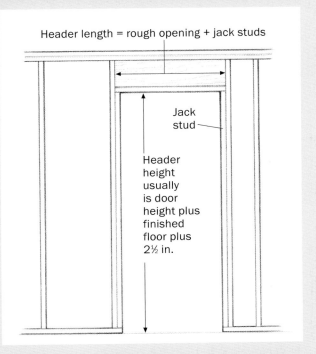

Header length = rough opening + jack studs

Jack stud

Header height usually is door height plus finished floor plus 2½ in.

These guidelines follow one fundamental rule of framing rough openings: Know your windows and doors. If you don't have the window or door on site, at the very least check the manufacturer's catalog to verify the rough-opening dimensions. Don't rely on the plans alone, and when in doubt, call the manufacturer.

The International Residential Code (IRC) specifies not only header size but also the number of jack studs for most common situations. While most windows and doors require just one jack stud at each end, long spans or extreme loads may call for two or more jack studs to increase the area bearing the load. If the loads on any header are concentrated over too small an area, the wood fibers at the ends of the header can be crushed. This can cause the header to drop, which in turn can crack drywall or, particu-

larly with patio doors and casement windows, cause the door or window to jam.

Header hangers, such as the Simpson Strong Tie® HH Series (see the photo on p. 9), can be used to eliminate jack studs altogether. I've used them in some remodeling situations when I needed to squeeze a patio door or a wide window into an existing wall that didn't have quite enough space for double jack studs. One jack and a Simpson HH Series hanger did the trick.

see the photo on p. 9

TIP

While most carpenters tend to think that more nails are a sign of good workmanship, headers need to be nailed with only one 10d common nail every 16 in. along each edge.

Headers: Sawn Lumber:
Traditional Material Still Carries the Load

DOUBLE 2X6 HEADER
Fine Homebuilding contributing editor Mike Guertin, whose day job is building houses in Rhode Island, uses the smallest allowable header depth to span the opening. While he must toenail cripples above each header, he argues that this header is the most economical. For starters, it conserves lumber. It also reduces the area of solid material in the wall, thus reducing thermal bridging. While the area is kept to a minimum, Guertin is also careful to keep the header to the outside of the wall, providing a gap that may be insulated with foam or wet-spray cellulose when the rest of the wall is insulated. A 2x3 nailed to the lower edge of the header provides attachment for trim.

DOUBLE 2X10 HEADER
A common header variant is used by North Carolina builder John Carroll. Built from double 2x10s, a stud-width nailer flat-framed along the bottom edge eases attaching sheathing or trim. Because this header is less than the full thickness of the wall, it allows for a piece of ½-in. foam to add a bit of insulation.

INSULATED HEADER
Custom builder David Crosby of Santa Fe, N.M., prefabs insulated headers from 2x10s and 2-in. extruded polystyrene foam. This option works particularly well in the cold mountains of northern New Mexico, where air temperatures can fall well below zero on winter nights. Even adding some ½-in foam to a double 2x header in a 2x4 wall improves thermal performance. While lumber in New Mexico is typically quite dry, due to the arid climate, Crosby ties the header to the jack stud with metal framing plates to control header shrinkage that could open gaps in the trim.

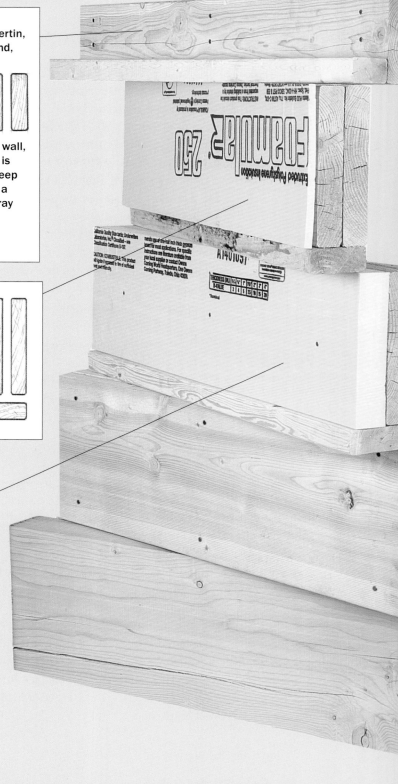

How Big a Header Do You Need?

Unless you're an engineer, the easiest way to size headers built with dimensional lumber is to check span charts, such as those in the IRC. The old rule of thumb is that headers made of double 2x stock can span safely in feet half their depth in inches. So by this rule, a double 2x12 can span 6 ft.

However, header spans vary not only with size, but also with lumber grade and species, with the width of the house, with your area's snow load, and with the number of floors to be supported. Consequently, the IRC provides 24 scenarios in which that double 2x12 header can span a range from 5 ft. 2 in. to 9 ft. 9 in. Check the code.

The Trouble with Cripples

Header size often is based on factors other than strength requirements. Many framers purposely oversize headers to avoid filling the space between the header and the double top plate with short studs (cripple studs, or

Hang Your Header

Sometimes, particularly in remodeling, there just isn't room for a jack stud. The IRC permits header hangers, such as Simpson's HH4 for 2x4 walls and HH6 for 2x6 walls, to substitute for single jack studs. These hangers are spiked with 16d common nails to the king stud.

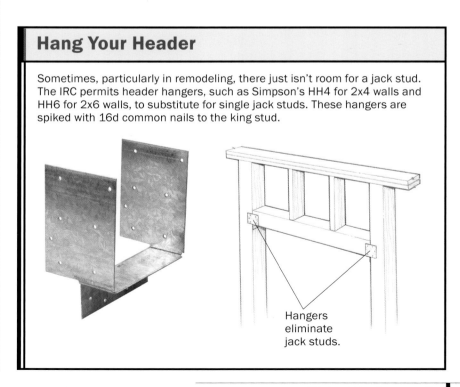

Hangers eliminate jack studs.

Sources

APA Engineered Wood Association
Nailed Structural-Use Panel and Lumber Beams
Available online
www.apawood.org

Simpson
4637 Chabot Dr., #200
Pleasanton, CA 94588
(800) 999-5099

Superior Wood
1301 Garfield Ave.
Superior, WI 54880
(800) 375-9992
www.swi-joist.com

TrusJoist MacMillan's Parallam
www.trusjoists.com

cripples). In a nominal 8-ft.-tall wall, a typical cripple stud measures 6 in. to 7 in. Such short studs are ungainly and are prone to splitting when they are nailed in place. Yet a double 2x12 header can be tucked beneath the double top plate, filling this miserable space and creating a proper opening for common 6-ft. 8-in. doors. Alternatively, builder John Carroll relies on a double 2x10 header with a 2x6 nailed flat along the bottom edge, which provides nailing for the head trim in a 2x6 wall.

However, such deep headers are oversize and add considerable cost, not to mention waste wood. Most window and door openings are only 3 ft. or so and might only require 2x6 headers. But perhaps the biggest drawback of wide lumber is that there's more of it to shrink. Framing lumber may have a moisture content of 19%. Once the heat is turned on, lumber typically dries to a moisture content of 9% to 11%, shrinking nominal 2x10s and 2x12s as much as ¼ in. across the grain. On the other hand, 2x6s might shrink only half that.

Shrinkage reduces the depth (or height) of the header; because the header is nailed firmly to the double top plate, a gap usually opens above the jack studs. As the header shrinks, it tends to pull up the head trim, which has been nailed to it, opening unsightly gaps in the casing and cracking any drywall seam spanning the header. The gap above the jack stud now means the header isn't supporting any load—until the first wet snowfall or heavy winds bring a crushing load to bear on the wall and push the gap closed, causing the top plates to sag, which can crack the drywall in the story above.

Shrinkage can be reduced using drier lumber, preferably at about 12%. However, lumber this dry may be difficult to find unless you can condition it yourself. As an alternative for spanning a large opening, consider using engineered materials (see photo on facing page). Laminated-veneer lumber (LVL) or parallel-strand lumber (PSL) shrinks much less than ordinary lumber.

If wide dimensional lumber is unavoidable, structural engineer Steve Smulski suggests that cracking can be minimized by not fastening the drywall to the header. This way, the header moves independently of the drywall, which then is less likely to crack. To prevent trim from moving as the header shrinks, attach the top piece of trim to the drywall only, using a minimal number of short, light-gauge finish nails and a bead of adhesive caulk.

Avoiding Condensation

In cold climates, uninsulated headers can create a thermal bridge. According to Smulski, the uninsulated header makes the wall section above windows and doors significantly colder than the rest of the wall (the same is true of solid-frame corners; see *Framing Corners* on pp. 44–49). When the difference between the inside and outside air temperatures is extreme, condensation may collect on these cold surfaces, and in the worst cases, mold and mildew may begin to grow.

To avoid condensation, it's important that any uninsulated header doesn't contact both the sheathing and the drywall. Unless you're building 2x4 exterior walls using full-thickness headers such as solid lumber or ones built out to 3½ in. with plywood, avoiding this situation is simple. Keep the header flush to the outside of the framing so that it contacts the sheathing. Because most other types of headers are narrower than the studs, there will be some airspace between the header and the drywall, which makes a dandy thermal break. In cold climates, a 2x10 insulated header, like the one used by David Crosby of Santa Fe, N. M., works well (see photo on p. 8). Another option that avoids solid lumber is a manufactured insulated I-beam header (see the photo on the facing page).

Clayton DeKorne is a carpenter and writer in Burlington, Vt. He is the author of Trim Carpentry and Built-Ins *(The Taunton Press, Inc., 2002).*

Headers Engineered Wood: Costs More, Does More

STORE-BOUGHT INSULATED HEADERS

Essentially a double-webbed I-joist with a chunk of rigid foam wedged in the middle, these engineered SW-II headers from Superior Wood Systems® offer insulation, strength, and light weight. You may have a hard time finding them locally, though, because they're new enough that distribution varies regionally. Price varies as well, depending on freight costs and markup. Hammond Lumber in Bangor, Maine, sells 14-ft. long, 5½-in. by 11¼-in. SW-II headers for about $90.

PARALLEL-STRAND LUMBER

Parallel-strand lumber, such as TrusJoist® MacMillan's Parallam, is available as stud-width stock. Performing much like the LVL above it, parallel-strand header stock is pricier than solid sawn lumber but 1½ times as stiff and 3 times as strong.

LAMINATED-VENEER LUMBER

Engineered lumber, shown in this header made from two pieces of 1¾-in. by 16-in. LVL (laminated-veneer lumber), offers some advantages over sawn lumber. While it's more expensive for smaller headers, engineered lumber is available in depths that can span distances sawn lumber simply isn't up to. And it's typically more stable, resulting in fewer drywall cracks.

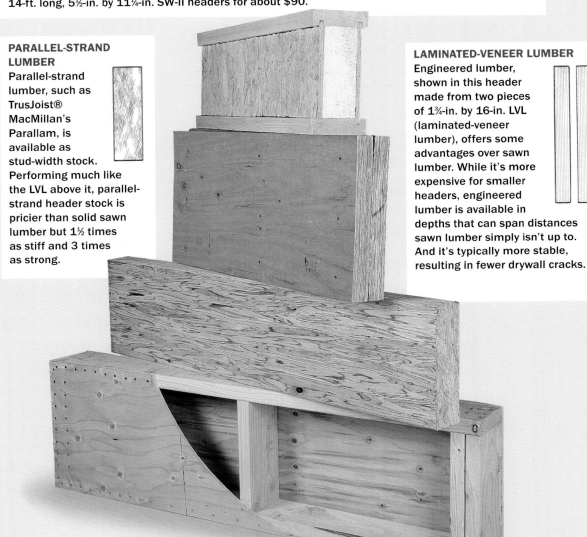

STRUCTURAL BOX BEAM

A box-beam header is a viable way to site-build long-span headers. A technical bulletin, *Nailed Structural-Use Panel and Lumber Beams,* outlines the design and fabrication of these stud and plywood beams. Because they end up being thicker than the studs, these plywood beams are better suited for long-span headers in an unfinished garage, where the exact thickness is a slight concern. For a 2x6 wall, though, you can make a box beam using 2x4 blocking and nominal ¾-in. structural plywood. A ½-in. furring strip brings such headers to the full wall thickness. And they can be stuffed with insulation.

Squaring and Leveling Mudsills

■ BY RICK ARNOLD AND MIKE GUERTIN

On one of our first framing jobs, the lead carpenter installed the mudsills by just lining them up with the outside edge of the foundation. It wasn't until the first-floor deck was framed and sheathed that we realized the foundation was 3 in. wider at one end, which made the whole platform miserably out of square. We battled problems from this little oversight all the way through the roof, and soon after we began looking for a new lead carpenter.

In the 15 or so years since that project, we've become a little fanatical about squaring and leveling our mudsills regardless of the scale or price range of the house. The reward for being finicky is a first-floor platform that is square, level, and built to the exact dimensions called for on the plans. This extra care that is taken at the beginning saves us time and headaches throughout the project.

Crew Members Must Communicate at All Times to Get Accurate Measurements

Measuring foundations is almost always a two-person job and may even involve three people, if more than one measuring tape is being used at one time. Constant communication between all crew members involved in a measurement is of utmost importance to the success of squaring and leveling.

We have an unwritten rule that the person on the beginning, or dummy, end of the measuring tape always calls out the measurement he is holding to the line as well as the color of that line—"5⅝, blue line," for instance. The person on the business end of the measuring tape always acknowledges his partner's call before recording the measurement.

To maintain the highest level of consistency and accuracy, we also insist that crew members never switch ends of the tape or

Parallel walls are lined up from the baseline. The two crew members in the background mark the same measurement from the baseline on the wall behind them. The crew member in the foreground moves the chalkline until it lines up with the marks determining the sill location for the garage wall.

Sill width determines baseline. After a rough check to verify the overall dimensions of the foundation, a baseline is established by measuring in the width of the sill from the edge of the concrete.

switch jobs with anyone else on the crew during the entire process. On past projects we wasted hours trying to figure out why dimensions didn't jibe only to discover that a crew member merely held the tape in the wrong spot and that his partner failed to check him.

Check the Foundation Right Away

We always square the foundation and snap lines for our mudsills right after the forms have been stripped (and before the foundation contractor is paid), even if we know that we won't begin framing for a while. Although totally unworkable foundations are rare, we have seen some foundation pours that were out of level as much as 3 in. in 40 ft. and some foundations that varied up to 12 in. from the specifications on the plan. Our crew can work comfortably with foundation tolerances that are within ¾ in. of square and ½ in. of level, and overall dimensions that are within ½ in. of the foundation plan.

We also doublecheck the foundation plan against the first-floor plan before lines are snapped. Simple features such as shelves for exterior brick veneer can have a way of throwing off foundation dimensions. Any deviation from the plan or discrepancy that

exceeds our tolerances adds cost to the project and needs to be addressed before we begin. The foundation that we will use to illustrate our methods is 40 ft. long and 30 ft. wide with an 8-ft. by 20-ft. breezeway that connects the house to a 24-ft. by 24-ft. garage. The rear foundation wall of the house is dropped 7 ft., and the gable-end foundation wall steps down with the grade.

After inspecting the foundation for any obvious problems, such as a large bump-out or a severe crown or dip, a couple of crew members check the overall foundation measurements. At the same time, other crew members sweep dirt or concrete debris off the top of the walls.

We install a double-2x6 mudsill system common to this part of southern New England, using pressure-treated lumber for the lower sill. With the double-mudsill system, leveling shims are inserted between the two layers, giving us a nice, tight seal against the concrete while providing a flat surface for the first-floor deck. We always check the width of a few pieces of the pressure-treated stock to determine the exact distance to set our chalkline back from the edge of the concrete. Most often this measurement is 5⅜ in.

Having inspected our foundation and found that it is close to the plan specifications, we choose the longest grade-level wall and mark 5⅜ in. from the outside of the concrete on each end (see the photo above). We snap a line between these marks in blue chalk to serve as a baseline. We snap our lines in blue chalk initially. Then, if the line needs to be adjusted for any reason, we switch to red. The crew has been instructed that a red line always supersedes a blue one.

The Rear Sills Are Lined Up Parallel to the Front

The next step is establishing a rear-wall line parallel to our baseline. Foundations that are poured all on one level are the easiest and quickest to deal with because lines and measurements can be made directly onto the foundation. One crew member holds the dummy end of the tape at 5⅝ in. over one end of the baseline while the other member with the business end of the tape marks the planned width of the house minus 5⅝ in. on the rear wall. The process is repeated at the other end, and a line is snapped on the rear wall between these marks.

As mentioned before, the rear wall of this particular foundation is 7 ft. lower than the front wall, and the end wall is stepped, which complicates the procedure slightly. We've devised a fixture that is nailed to the lower foundation corner and that holds a dry string (in place of the chalkline) at the height of the grade-level portion of the foundation (see the top right photo on p. 16). Instead of marking and snapping a chalkline on the rear foundation wall, we run a dry string at the same elevation as the front wall. This string is positioned 29 ft. 6⅜ in. from the baseline (30 ft. for the width of the house minus 5⅝ in. for the width of the sill). Because the rear wall of the garage happens to be in line with the rear of the house foundation, we extend the dry string all the way through to the gable end of the garage and drive a nail into the concrete there to anchor the string in position. This dry string will remain in place as a reference line until we've finished installing the sills.

We establish the parallel line for the front wall of the garage by measuring 6 ft. from our baseline on the two walls that run perpendicular to the front wall (see the photo on p. 13). We extend a chalkline from the 6-ft. mark on the end wall of the house across the front wall of the garage. The line is then moved until it aligns with the 6-ft. mark on the intermediate perpendicular wall. Before the line is snapped, we secure it and verify that it is parallel to the dry line at the rear wall of the garage by measuring between the two. If our measurements are off slightly, we tweak the line at the end of

the garage to compensate. When we're satisfied, we snap the line for the garage wall in blue. We can now locate and snap any other parallel lines, such as the front wall of the breezeway, by referencing one of the snapped lines or the dry string.

Perpendicular Lines Are Located by Simple Geometry

We have just established the lines for our front and rear walls. The distance between these lines is the length of our perpendicular walls. Next we locate the corner points that will give us the lengths of our front and rear walls as well as the placement of perpendicular walls, and we can begin to square the foundation.

When we made a rough measurement of the foundation earlier, we determined that the actual length of the front wall along our baseline was close to the specified length of 40 ft. So next we mark 5⅝ in. in from the outside of the concrete at one end of our baseline. One crew member holds the tape at 5⅝ in. on that mark while a second pulls the tape along the wall and marks the baseline at 39 ft. 6⅜ in., or 5⅝ in. back from the total length of the wall.

Our next step is establishing a perpendicular line for the gable end of the house exactly 90° to the baseline. In the past we tried the 3-4-5 right-triangle method, which got us close but not perfect. We used right-angle prisms, but we found them to be slow and hard to work with. The Pythagorean theorem also works fine, but the calculations have to be precise. Also, figuring in the 5⅝ in. setback on top of all that will befuddle even the most mathematically inclined. Our latest method has outperformed all others in simplicity and speed.

Three People + Two 100-ft. Tapes = One Square Foundation

There are actually two variations to our method. The first and most efficient method requires three people and two 100-ft. tapes.

Two crew members hold the 2-in. line of their tapes on the corner marks at each end of the front-wall baseline. We use the 2-in. mark because it is usually the first whole-inch mark on a 100-ft. tape; it also gives the crew member plenty to hold on to when the tape is being stretched tight. The third person holds the business end of both tapes near the middle of the line or, in this case, the dry string on the opposite wall. This person crosses the two tapes and moves left or right

Two tapes locate the mid-point. A crew member crosses two tapes that are being stretched from the ends of the baseline. A small piece of twine is tied on the dry string where the two tapes meet at exactly the same length. This point marks the center of the rear wall.

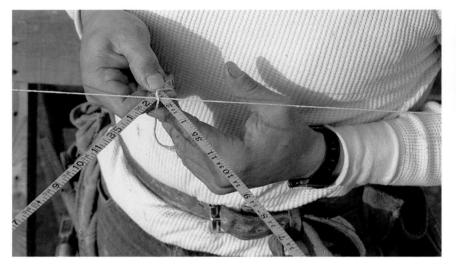

Dry strings are used where the foundation drops. To guarantee square mudsills on the dropped foundation, the crew projects the measurements to dry strings held at the same level as the rest of the foundation. The homemade device for holding the dry strings has an angle iron that is nailed into the foundation and a telescoping pipe to allow the crew to adjust the height of the strings.

Diagonal measurements are the final check for square. After the corners are located on the rear wall, the crew measures between them and the baseline corners. If the measuring procedures have been followed carefully, the two diagonal measurements should be within ⅛ in.

along the line until the measurements on the two tapes match exactly (see the left photo on the facing page). This point indicates the exact center of the rear wall, and it's marked either with a pencil line on the foundation or a piece of twine tied around the dry string (an alligator clip from an electronics-supply store also works well to mark a point on a dry string).

From the midpoint we measure half the length of the wall minus the width of the sill in each direction to get our inside-corner marks (see the right photo on the facing page). For insurance we doublecheck the overall length of the rear wall. Now, as a final check for square, we measure diagonally from corner to corner on the foundation (see the bottom photo on the facing page). If we've done our job properly, those measurements should be within ⅛ in.

Two Crew Members and One Tape Take a Little Longer

If there are only two crew members or just one 100-ft. tape available, we use a modified method that's a little slower but works just as well as the first system. We mark the length of our baseline just as before. Then one person holds the tape at 2 in. on one end of the line.

Instead of crossing two tapes, the guy on the business end stretches the single tape across the opposite parallel line near the midpoint and picks the closest 1-ft. increment on the tape. For our purposes we'll call that measurement 42 ft. The crew member on the business end then moves the tape along the line and marks where the 42-ft. mark on the tape intersects with the chalk-line or dry string. The dummy end of the tape is then moved to the mark at the opposite end of the baseline, and the tape is held at the same 2-in. point. The business end again marks the point where the 42-ft. mark on the tape intersects with the line. The midpoint between these two marks should be

A plumb bob transfers the corner point to the wall below. The intersection of the two dry strings is the exact corner of the sill layout. That point, as well as any others needed to snap chalk-lines, is found by dropping a plumb line from the dry string.

the midpoint of the wall. Just as before, we measure to the left and to the right of this midpoint half the length of the wall, again minus the width of our sills, to locate our corner points, and again we confirm overall squareness with diagonal measurements.

With both methods, once we're sure that we have a perfect rectangle, we snap lines for the perpendicular walls between the corner points on our front and rear walls. From those lines, we can measure and snap any other lines that are perpendicular to our baseline, including the gable-end wall of the garage.

Both rear-corner points of this foundation happen to be "in the air" because of the drops in the foundation. On the corner where our dry-string fixture is mounted, we indicate the line of the gable-end wall using another dry string instead of a snapped line. The intersection of the two dry strings tied to our fixture is our exact corner point (see

the photo on p. 17). Starting at this point, we drop a plumb bob down to the lower foundation walls at enough locations to let us snap lines. But on a windy day even the tightest dry string will tend to move a bit. And even the slightest breeze can make using a plumb bob impractical. If the wind turns our plumb bob into a pendulum, we reluctantly use a 4-ft. level in its place.

Water Levels Are the Most Accurate Tools for Leveling Sills

For years we used a builder's transit to set our sills level, and it worked fine most of the time. We still use one occasionally if it is the best-suited tool. However, transits are delicate and vulnerable instruments, particularly around framing crews on job sites. Invariably, the transit gets knocked over or ends up bouncing around in the back of someone's pickup. Consequently, our transits seemed to spend more time in the shop being adjusted than they spent out in the field.

The tool we've come to depend on for leveling our mudsills is the good, old-fashioned, low-tech water level. We've been accused of being too cheap to buy a transit, and skeptics doubt the accuracy of our water-filled plastic hose. But our water level consistently outperforms the transit for both speed and accuracy. In fact, we have used our water level to inform the foundation contractor that his transit needs calibration.

We first pick a corner of the foundation and mark 1½ in. down from the top of the concrete (see the photo at left). After checking the plastic hose for air bubbles and making sure the fluid level in both ends is equal, one crew member, designated as the lead person, raises or lowers the hose until the water level matches his starting mark while another crew member on the other end of the hose marks the level of his corner at the lead's command (see the photo on the facing page). For the sake of consistency, we

Leveling the foundation begins with a reference point. A crew member makes a mark 1½ in. down on one corner of the foundation. From this point the crew uses a water level (photo facing page) and marks every corner. A level line between the marks will help locate places in the foundation that might be out of level.

A water level is quicker, easier to use, and more accurate than a transit. Having tested many kinds of leveling devices, including builder's transits, this crew's tool of choice is a water level. The tool requires no calibration and holds up well under the rigors of house framing.

always make our mark at the bottom of the meniscus (the concave shape of the water surface inside the hose).

We try to mark as many corners of the foundation as our length of hose allows from a single reference point. If a corner is beyond the reach of the hose, the lead person repositions himself at the farthest mark, and the process resumes.

On some foundations it is necessary for the lead person to move four or five times to catch all the corners of the foundation. We mark the entire grade level of the foundation and always work our way back to our starting corner to check ourselves. We are usually within ⅛ in., which is an acceptable tolerance.

If there is a drop or a step in the foundation, we mark the level on the wall just before the drop. Next we measure the drop and round to the nearest inch. We then measure that distance down from the upper-level mark and make a new lower mark on the dropped wall. We continue the leveling process from this point, marking all the dropped foundation walls at each corner until the wall elevation returns to the original level. At this point the measurement between the upper and lower levels should be within ⅛ in. of the original drop measurement.

After making level marks around the entire foundation, we go back and snap lines between our marks. Sometimes we have to scrape off excess concrete at the form-panel seams if it interferes with the chalkline. After the level line is snapped, a crew member takes measurements from the top of the concrete to the chalkline at random points around the foundation. This process gives us an idea of any areas where we'll have to adjust the level of the sills.

Nuts on Foundation Bolts Start Out Only Finger-Tight

Once all of our lines are snapped, we can install the sills. We cut the lower sill stock to length for each section of foundation and line it up on the inside of the chalkline (see the photo on p. 20). Next, we locate the bolt holes with a homemade tool made from a piece of metal with a U-shape on one end and a hole drilled 5⅝ in. back from the U. We butt the U against the bolt with the tool squared to the sill stock by eye and mark the bolt location through the hole on the other end of the tool. The holes we drill in the mudsills are oversize so that we can adjust the sills to the chalklines once they're in place.

We roll out sill seal just before dropping the sills over the bolts. The lower sill is held in place with masonry nails until the upper sill can be marked, drilled, and set on top. We cut the upper 2x6 sills so that the corners cross lap the lower sills. We also try to overlap any butt seams in the upper and lower sills by at least 4 ft. to make straightening bowed sill stock an easier job. We avoid landing seams over windows or bulkhead openings. We extend upper sills beyond any foundation drops by at least 4 ft. to tie into the kneewall below.

In most cases the kiln-dried lumber we use for the upper sill is narrower than the pressure-treated sill on the bottom. In order to maintain the proper outside dimensions of the house framing, we keep the inside of the bottom sill flush with the chalkline on the foundation, and we keep the outside of the upper sill flush with outside of the lower sill. We tack the upper sill in place with a couple of nails every few feet, and we put the nuts and washers on the foundation bolts only finger-tight at first in case shimming is necessary.

A simple jig locates the bolt holes. With the sill stock lined up on the inside of the chalkline, a jig with a U-shaped end is held against the bolt. The bolt-hole location is marked through a hole 5⅝ in. from the U.

Shims between the Sills Bring Them up to Level

Most of the foundations we work on are within ¼ in. from the highest point to the lowest point; and by the time we lay the sills on top of the sill seal, these differences are negligible. When we do encounter a more significant dip in the foundation, we use flat bars to pry the sills apart, and we insert shims between the sills to bring them up to level (see the photo above). The nails we used to tack the two sills together now hold them apart while we slip in the shim shingles. We try to place the shims directly beneath the joist location for the best support of the platform.

If we find that an entire wall is low by ¼ in. or more, we rip 5½-in. strips of the appropriate thickness plywood and sandwich them between the two sills. Occasionally, we encounter a hump in a foundation. Rather than shim all of the sills up to this level of the hump, we make the adjustment

later by scribing the rim joist and notching the joists slightly as long as the hump isn't huge. This procedure is preferable to shimming the sills around the entire perimeter of the foundation.

Once the shimming is complete, we tighten the nuts, but only snug so we don't create additional dips in the sills. We complete the installation by nailing the top and bottom sills together according to the local code.

As a final note, the entire process of squaring and leveling a foundation usually takes three crew members about two hours. It takes the same three guys another two hours to drill, shim, and nail the sills in place. Expect these methods to take a bit longer at first, but with practice they'll become quicker and easier. Also, that level line snapped around the foundation will come in handy later on for orienting the siding.

Shims correct an out-of-level foundation wall. If there are dips in the foundation, the two sills are pried apart with a flat bar. The nails used to tack the upper sill in place now serve to hold the two sills apart while shims are inserted beneath the future joist layout.

Rick Arnold and Mike Guertin are builders, remodelers, and contributing editors to Fine Homebuilding. *Rick is the author of* Working with Concrete *(2003) and Mike is the author of* Roofing with Asphalt Shingles *(2002), both published by The Taunton Press, Inc.*

Cutting Multiples

■ BY LARRY HAUN

One thing that I've noticed in the years I've been a carpenter and teacher is that cutting multiple pieces can be a terrible time-waster. If, for instance, you asked beginning carpenters to cut 100 blocks and didn't give them any further instruction, it would take them about 100 minutes to do the job. That's because most people tend to cut one block at a time. And it takes about a minute to find a piece of wood, measure it for length, mark it, and then make the cut. That's fine if you have one or two blocks to cut, but not if you have 100.

On most any job there are numerous occasions when carpenters will need piles of blocks, cripples, headers, trimmers, or studs all cut to the same length. Some builders make a cutting list that contains the size, the length, and the number of these items and then submit the list to their lumber companies along with the rest of the order. Large lumber companies often have gang saws, and with the press of a button, a saw operator can make a pallet of blocks in no time. The blocks can be shipped to the job site with the rest of the order.

Most of us, though, don't operate that way. When we need a rack of cripples, we set up right in our work area and cut them. There are several methods for cutting multiple pieces that are a lot faster than cutting them one at a time. The two keys are: Cut more than one board at a time, which is called gang-cutting, and don't measure each board individually.

Use a Radial-Arm Saw and a Stop Block

For many builders, the radial-arm saw is the preferred tool for gang-cutting wood to length. Some carpenters mount their radial-arm saw right on the back of a pickup so that the tool is readily available. I have mine mounted on its own trailer so that the saw can be pulled from job to job.

To cut multiple pieces with the radial-arm saw, I build a simple table out of a 14-ft.- or 16-ft.-long 2x12 (or two 2x6s) and nail a 2x4 fence to the back side. To make repetitive cuts to the same length, all you have to do is attach a stop block to the table at the correct

Why move the pile? Studs, blocks, and cripples also can be cut right on the lumber pile. The author starts by flushing up the ends of the top layer of 2xs. He snaps a line across the pile at the right length, sets his saw to 1½ in. deep, and makes the cut.

distance from the blade (see the photo at right). With a stop block in place, you can feed in several 2xs at a time on edge and turn out a pile of blocks or cripples in short order because you're not stopping to measure and mark each piece. If a radial-arm saw isn't available, you can do the same thing with a power miter saw. The stop may be screwed, nailed, or clamped to the worktable. If you have many cuts to make, be sure the stop block is well secured so that it isn't gradually forced out of position when you push the end of a 2x against it.

It pays to watch for sawdust that gets trapped between the stop block and the 2x you are cutting because your cuts can be thrown off by it. You can avoid the problem by cutting a chamfer, or bevel, on the bottom edge of the stop block so that sawdust is pushed out of the way.

Cutting blocks on the radial-arm saw. Using a radial-arm saw is a fast way to cut multiple pieces on a job site. Several 2xs can be cut at the same time, and an adjustable stop block makes it unnecessary to measure stock for each cut. A bevel on the bottom edge of the wooden stop block helps prevent a buildup of sawdust, which will throw off the accuracy of the cut.

Cut Right on the Lumber Pile

For many builders, the circular saw may be the only saw available on the job site, and it can be used to cut multiple pieces right on the lumber pile. Usually, 2x stock is delivered in bundles or lifts with pieces lying flat; the material can be cut before it's taken off the pile. Before cutting the pieces to length, you need to flush up one end so that all the blocks or studs will be the same length. This can be done easily by holding the edge of a straight stud against one end of the top layer and pushing all the 2xs to a straight line. If the material is too heavy to push, you can

stick the claws of your hammer into them and pull the 2xs against the straightedge. Once the 2xs are even at one end, you can measure down the two outside pieces to the point where the cut should be made and snap a line across the pile. Then set the saw to cut 1½ in. deep and make the cut (see the top photo on p. 23).

Rack Up Blocks to Cut All at Once

Once a job is underway, there often is scrap material around that you will want to use up. Let's say you need 60 cripples, each cut 3 ft. long. Gather up pieces of 2x scrap and

Pulling to a line. When gang-cutting 2x4s on edge, the author starts by pulling the stock to a straightedge, in this case a straight 2x4, with the claws of his hammer.

Measure once, cut twice. The author snaps a line between marks on the two outside 2x4s and then cuts on the line with the blade of his saw at full depth. After the first cut has been made, each 2x4 is picked up in turn, and the cut completed. The stock does not have to be marked again.

Making small blocks. If the blocks are short, many of them may be made from a small stack of 2x scrap. The author snaps a series of lines across the scrap and makes the cuts, keeping the blade to the same side of the line each time so that the blocks are the same length.

line them up, on edge, against a bottom sill or another straightedge on the job (see the top photo on the facing page). Measure up 3 ft. from the flush end and snap a chalkline across the entire line of 2xs. You can cut the full depth of the blade along the line (see the bottom left photo on the facing page) and then pick up each piece individually to finish the cut (see the bottom right photo on the facing page). You won't have to mark the studs a second time. If you only have a few to cut, it is easier to lay them flat on the floor and make the cut in one pass.

This technique also works well when making a lot of short blocks (see the photo above). If the scrap pieces of 2x are long enough, you can snap a number of lines across them at the right spacing and then make a number of cuts with your saw with-out further measuring or marking. Just remember to keep your blade on the same side of the chalkline each time so that the blocks are the same length.

Lay Out Multiples with a Framing Square

You can also use your framing square to speed the cutting of blocks. I frequently need a number of lap or eaves blocks to fit between joists or rafters. When scrap pieces are not available, it is easier to lay out and cut the blocks from full-length stock right on the deck than it is trying to muscle 2x10s or 2x12s onto a saw table. If you are cutting 14½-in. blocks (the length that fits between rafters or joists 16 in. o. c.), align the 14½-in. mark on the inside of the blade of the

Sources

**Muskegon
Power Tools**
2357 Whitehall Rd.
N. Muskegon, MI
49445
(800) 635-5465
www.linearlink.com

Prazi USA
118 Long Pond Rd.
Unit G
Plymouth, MA 02360
(800) 262-0211
www.praziusa.com

Skip the tape. When cutting short lengths of blocking from a long 2x, there's no need to measure and square each block separately. Instead, the author uses his framing square to mark off blocks quickly. He aligns the end of the 2x with the correct measurement on the inside of the square's blade, uses the tongue to mark a square line across the 2x, and then moves the square along the 2x to repeat the process.

Big saw, big cut. A large-capacity beam saw is capable of cutting 2x4s or 2x6s on edge. The author just lines up a stack of 2xs, snaps a line and makes the cut. No second cut is needed. A 2x4 spacer prevents the saw from cutting the plywood floor.

square with the end of the 2x. Then draw a line across the 2x using the inside of the tongue of the square as your guide. Now move the 14½-in. mark to the line and repeat the process (see the photo at left). Using this method, you can work your way down a 2x quickly. When it's time to cut the blocks, hold the sawblade to the same side of the line each time to ensure that each block is the same length.

Get a Bigger Saw

A beam saw can cut through a 2x6 on edge and can also be used to make the ridge cut when gang-cutting common rafters. A beam saw is just an oversized circular saw; my Makita® has a 16-in. blade. So if I'm cutting blocks from 2x4 or 2x6 stock on edge, the entire cut can be made in a single pass. In this case, I place a flat 2x under the stock near the chalkline to hold the 2x material away from the deck (see the photo below). A little paraffin on the blade makes the cut go easier.

If you don't have a beam saw and don't want to invest in one, a chainsaw attachment will increase the capacity of your circular saw. One kind is the Prazi Beam Cutter™, which the manufacturer says can be put on and taken off in a few minutes. The company makes models that fit either a worm-drive circular saw or a sidewinder. Another brand is the Linear Link VCS-12 from Muskegon Power Tools. The Linear Link can be purchased either as a complete saw or as a kit to convert your worm-drive, although it's not sold as a quick-change accessory. Both the Linear Link and the Prazi increase the cutting capacity of your saw to 1 ft. at 90°. This type of saw is especially useful when gang-cutting the ridge cut on wide rafters.

Larry Haun is the author of Habitat for Humanity: How to Build a House (2002), *published by The Taunton Press, Inc. He lives in Coos Bay, Oregon.*

Framing with Steel for the First Time

■ BY ROBERT MCCULLOUGH

Until two years ago, I'd spent my construction career building houses of wood. Then I got a tempting offer. My father-in-law, architect Berle Pilsk, wanted me to build his new house at Sea Ranch, Calif. The thought of spending a year living on the northern California coast and building a house in a redwood grove was enticing. The only hitch: The house was to be of steel.

Berle is convinced that steel-frame houses represent the next advance in residential construction. A steel frame doesn't rot, insects won't eat it, it won't burn, it resists earthquakes well, the parts are of uniform dimension, and—perhaps best of all—at this writing the cost of steel components is substantially less than comparable wood components on the northern California coast.

But I was skeptical. I like working with wood. It smells good, and it's easy to cut, shape, and fasten. So before I took on the job, I spent a lot of time with Berle, going over the hypothetical construction of the house. I found a couple of steel houses that were under construction and studied them. I learned that a steel-frame house is essentially the same as a stick-frame house—the

Posts can be assembled in place. The author screws a track onto a pair of studs to complete a built-up post. To his right, a pair of cantilevered headers meets at an outside corner. The headers are stuffed with insulation and anchored to one another with steel straps.

parts are just made of different materials. But there are some significant differences that you should be aware of if you're familiar with wood construction and if you're contemplating your first steel-framing project. For information on specific construction details, get in touch with the American Iron and Steel Institute. The group's technical-data brochure, *Low-Rise Residential Construction Details* ($20), is filled with easy-to-decipher assembly drawings. What's more, that phone number will hook you up with their technical-advice hot line.

A 2x6 Is Really 6 in. Wide

Steel-framing members consist of two basic components that are C-shaped in section, with a couple of important differences. Studs, joists, and rafters are made with members that have flanges folded inward about ¼ in. at their open corners (see the top photo on p. 30). These folds, while almost insignificant dimensionally, add stiffness to the members and make it easy for a stud to stand vertically. Studs come with prepunched holes in their webs for electrical conduits. Joists and rafters can have solid webs or be prepunched.

The other basic components are tracks. They have solid webs and lack the folded corners on the legs. Tracks work both as sill plates and top plates, and as part of posts or headers when combined with studs. Tracks also can be used for blocking and backing.

Like wood components, studs, joists, rafters, and tracks come in various dimensions that differ in regular increments. But unlike wood, the dimensions are a net figure. In other words, 6 in. means 6 in. Studs are measured from their outside dimensions, and tracks are measured from the inside of their legs. So a 6-in. stud fits snugly into the track as shown in the photo. Self-tapping screws driven through the legs of the track and the legs of the stud hold the assembly together.

Steel-framing members come in many different sizes and gauges. We were able to order and receive floor joists and rafters in excess of 30 ft. They were all the same length, and they were all perfectly straight. There is no sorting through the pile looking for the "perfect timber," although I must confess to picking up a stud from time to time and absentmindedly sighting down its length. Old habits are hard to break.

Steel components are surprisingly light for their strength. Without much difficulty, one person can carry a 30-ft. rafter. Studs are shipped nested together in bundles of 10. One person can pick up and carry a bundle of 10-ft. studs with relative ease. They don't take up much space, and it doesn't matter how long they sit. They will never dry, warp, split, rot, or burn.

I had no problem with getting my hands on the stuff. Deliveries were prompt and on schedule, and our supplier needed a minimum of advance notice. The steel usually comes on a large flatbed with many small bundles banded together into several large and heavy bundles. The driver can't just drop the load as with lumber because steel distorts and bends when it hits the ground. A forklift is the best tool for unloading the material. In addition to making quick work of the job, a forklift allows you to keep large bundles together until you need the materials.

By the way, our steel came coated with a water-based lubricant that made it tricky to handle. Gloves are required. Once the steel sits out in the weather, it loses the slippery quality, but gloves are always a good idea. A word to the wise: When ordering, order carefully because you can't run down to the lumberyard and pick up a few more sticks—yet.

One of the attractive things about framing in steel is its amazing strength. You can increase the strength, and hence the load-bearing capabilities of the member, simply by increasing the thickness, or gauge, of the metal. You don't have to increase the dimensions of the member. When you increase the thickness of a steel member, the gauge number gets smaller. For example, a 12-ga. stud is beefier than a 20-ga. stud.

Screws Hold It All Together

The numbering system works the opposite way for the screws that hold a steel frame together. A #8 screw is much smaller and does not provide as much strength as a #14 screw.

Screws have either Phillips-head recesses, square-drive recesses, or hexagonal heads. We used all three. Phillips and square-drive screws work best for thinner materials. When we had to screw through anything thicker than 14 ga., we used hex-head screws because it's tough to deform a hexagonal screw head, even under the constant, intense torque it takes to get a screw into thick sheet metal. It is important—almost mandatory—to keep a hex-head screw perpendicular to the material when you're driving it home. If you angle a hex-head screw as it is driven, it will simply spin out of the drive socket. A Phillips-head screw, on the other hand, can be angled into the work and still be driven, which allows you to get in some tight places. Pan-head screws are designed to be used in places that will be covered with drywall, where the fatter hex-head screws would cause a bulge.

Screwing steel-framing components to one another is not difficult. It is, however, time-consuming. For example, the basic screw for anchoring a stud to a track on our job was the #8, ½-in. pan-head self-drilling screw (see the middle photo on p. 30). Over the course of building this house, we went through 20,000 of these screws. Let's say we dropped 1,000 on the ground. This leaves 19,000 screws. On the average, it takes about 30 seconds to drive one of these screws. Convert 9,500 minutes into workdays, and you get almost 20 eight-hour days.

A New Set of Tools

You can get material precut to specific lengths, but we decided to cut the components on site because of the intricacies of the house. The cut-off saw (see the photo below) is the best tool for the job. After researching the field, I concluded that all the saws are pretty much the same and ended up buying the Makita.

Although the saws are similar, there is a big difference in the blades. After trying every available metal-cutting blade we could find, we concluded that the ones made by Norton lasted the longest. On a day of cutting, it's easy to go through a couple of 14-in. sawblades.

Take the studs to the saw. A cut-off saw with a composition blade is the standard method of cutting steel-framing components. Cutting sheet metal this way demands adequate safety protection.

Components and Fasteners

The basic components in a steel-frame house are C-shaped in section. As shown in the top photo, a stud nests in a track. Note how the legs of the stud curl inward, strengthening the form. The prepunched hole in the stud is for wiring. In the middle, a built-up post is composed of two studs and two tracks. The part on the right is a hat channel. It's typically used for purlins.

Be sure to choose the right screw for the job. Most steel-framing screws have self-drilling tips that eliminate the need for drilling a pilot hole (see the bottom photo). Phillips-head and square-drive screws are good for 20-ga. and thinner metal. Hex-head screws are best for thicker metal. Use the wing-tip screws for attaching wood to metal.

1. #14, 1¼-in. hex washer-head screw.
2. #12, 1-in. hex washer-head screw.
3. 2¼-in. Phillips bugle-head screw.
4. 1⅝-in. square-drive flathead trim screw.
5. #8, ½-in. Phillips pan-head screw.
6. #10, 1-in. hex washer-head screw.
7. #12, 2½-in. Phillips flat countersunk-head screw with wings.
8. #10, 1½-in. Phillips flat wafer-head screw with wings.
9. #8, 1-in. Phillips pan-head screw.

You can drive a self-tapping screw (the pointy tip on the left in the bottom photo) into the thinner steel components. If the steel is thicker than 20-ga., however, use a fastener with the self-drilling-type tip on the right. The screw in the center, which is used to affix wood to metal, has a self-drilling tip with little wings between the tip and the threads. The wings carve the hole in wood, then break off when they encounter steel.

Framing Members

Fasteners

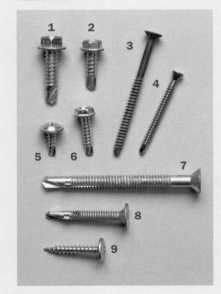

Screw Tips

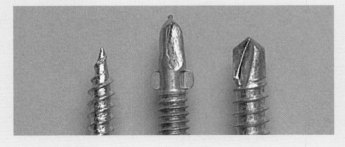

Cutting metal tracks and studs is a noisy job that produces steel slivers that can get in your eyes and clouds of acrid smoke that can sting your lungs. Protect yourself with earmuffs or earplugs, eye goggles, and a respirator. Also, have a first-aid kit with plenty of Band-Aids®, antibiotic ointment, and eye wash. It is important to wear the eye protection because a metal sliver is nothing like a wood one. A steel sliver tends to stay in the eye, where it immediately starts to rust.

We used Porter-Cable® screwguns for assembling the components and a Bosch® battery-powered drill with a long extension to reach the nearly inaccessible places that needed screws (a cordless drill seems to work better than a standard drill if you can't hold the tool perpendicular to the work).

I never did find a store-bought hex-head driver for the #10s that would magnetically hold the screw. The head depth of the #10 is shallower than the #12, so the magnet doesn't quite engage the head of the screw. We solved the problem by adding a thin magnet to the driver socket.

Here's the lineup of tools for steel framing that I carry in my belt: two large Vise-Grip® C-clamps, spare Phillips and hex-head screwdrivers, a stringline, a plumb bob, a magnetic torpedo level, end nips for changing the driver bits in my screwgun and removing backed-out screws, a utility chisel, three pairs of metal snips (straight, right-hand and left-hand), a 4-in-1 screwdriver, a utility knife, a tape measure, a speed square, my cat's paw, and, finally, my hammer, for balance if nothing else. I'd say the whole kit weighs about 25 lb.

The Layout Has to Be Impeccable

A steel house is put together in small pieces, just like the typical platform-frame house of wood. The foundations are the same for wood or steel, but with steel it is important to trowel smooth the top of the foundation because the steel track is not as forgiving as a wood mudsill atop a layer of sill sealer. We used traditional ⅝-in. foundation bolts for the typical stretch of foundation. Where the

The view from the crawl-space. Joists at 4 ft. o. c. carry the corrugated metal deck of the main floor. Each joist is carried by a pair of studs. At the pony wall in the background, web stiffeners midway between the joists carry the loads from the walls above. Note how the joists are blocked at the rim tracks by short sections of steel studs and at midspan by blocking made of steel studs.

engineer called for heavier connections to the foundation, we used ¼-in. steel plates affixed to the foundation with ⅞-in. bolts. The plates were then connected to the frame by way of diagonal braces made of 16-ga. steel.

One of our first problems to solve was how to cut the holes in the track for the foundation bolts. At first I used a bimetal hole saw, but I found this to be difficult and sometimes painful. A hole saw has a tendency to bind in the kerf and then jerk your wrist. I finally found a stepped drill bit, which is cone-shaped and starts small enough not to need a pilot hole but ends up big enough to create a 1-in. hole. This tool also came in handy when it was time to install plumbing and electrical. Although the studs came pre-punched, we sometimes needed to make holes in built-up posts and headers to run wires and pipes.

Accurate layout of framing members is important no matter what the material, but with steel layout, accuracy takes on greater importance. Rafters must be over either a post or a double stud. If the house is more than one story tall, posts and studs must bear on a plate that is supported either by a joist or a short piece of stud called a web stiffener placed in the joist track directly under the post or stud (see the photo on p. 31). These loads must be transferred to the foundation by corresponding posts and studs in the lower floors. So when we were laying out first-floor walls, we were also laying out roof framing.

Frame the Walls in Place

A carpenter typically lays out the parts of a wood wall on the subfloor, frames the wall in the horizontal position, and then lifts it into place. A steel-frame wall requires that the screws be driven from both sides of the track into the legs of the stud. So we framed the walls, which have their studs on 24-in. centers, in place to gain access to the other side (for another approach, see the sidebar on pp. 34–35).

After marking the position of the stud (pencils worked fine), we placed a stud in the track. Then we clamped it in place with the Vise-Grip C-clamp and tapped the stud firmly downward to make sure it was seated correctly. This is an important step. The American Iron and Steel Institute recommends a gap of no more than 1/16 in. between a stud and its track. If the gap is larger, the screws end up as the bearing points.

After tapping the stud down, we ran the appropriate screw through the track and into the leg of the stud. Then we clamped the other side of the stud and screwed it to the track. For bearing walls, we found it easiest to install all the studs and then come back and add the top track. Walls that intersect at corners are attached with screws through the abutting studs and by straps that wrap around the tracks at the top of the wall.

Partition walls were easier to build by positioning the top and bottom tracks and then filling in the studs. This step should be done only with nonbearing walls because it's tough to make sure there aren't gaps larger than 1/16 in. between studs and tracks. Because we were building on a sloping site, we had to erect pony walls (sometimes called cripple walls or jack walls) of various heights to establish a level top plate. Then we were ready to lay out our floor. Incidentally, we sprayed the cut ends of any framing members in the crawl space with some zinc-rich Rust-oleum® paint.

Rolling out steel joists goes really fast. First, we installed a rim track (a 20-ga. track stood on end) on top of the pony walls and then screwed the joists to the track on 48-in. centers. Halfway between the joists we installed web stiffeners in the track to pick up the load of the studs to come.

We also installed web stiffeners adjacent to each joist, screwing into the side of the joist as well as into the inside of the rim track. The stiffeners, like blocking, supported the sides of the joists and added rigidity to the rim track.

A Metal Deck Supports a Slab Floor

At this point, most houses would be ready for a subfloor. But our project has a radiant-slab concrete floor poured over a metal deck. So our next step was to install a 20-ga. metal angle around the inside perimeter of the walls (see the photo below). Called a closure strip, this metal angle acts as a flange that supports the metal deck at the edges while simultaneously working as a screed for the concrete and a strap tie at the corners to hold the wall tracks together.

Once the closure strip was installed, we laid the 3-ft. by 12-ft. pieces of 20-ga. deck-

This floor deck hangs on a closure strip. A metal angle called a closure strip supports the edges of the corrugated floor decking and acts as a screed to control the concrete's thickness. In this photo, you can see the closure strip at the outside corner, just inside the overlapping tracks that secure the intersecting walls.

ing perpendicular to the joists. The corrugations in the decking nest inside one another, and they overlap one corrugation at their edges. This overlap has to be crimped by a tool that looks like a big pair of bolt cutters. Called button-punching, this operation goes quickly once you have the tool. It took an hour to do the crimps and two days to find and fetch the tool from the rental yard.

If the sections of metal decking, or pans, needed to be cut to length, we used a circular saw fitted with an 8½-in. Norton blade. We affixed the decking to the joists and the closure strips with screws. Screwing the pans to the floor joists really tied the whole platform together, giving us a rigid deck for the main floor of the house. By the way, the light coming off the deck was blinding. We all had to break out the tinted safety glasses when the sun cleared the trees.

If you have occasion to install a metal-pan deck, here are a few things to consider: First, the corrugations in the deck make it tough to keep clean. Debris can be swept into piles along the flutes, but you can't get a dustpan in there. Make sure to have a vacuum on hand. Rain on an unswept metal deck makes a real mess that's tough to clean up. Also, a metal deck isn't much fun to walk on. In our case, the slab was going to be stained and polished to become the finished floor. So we waited until the end of the project to pour the slab. If the slab were to be covered with some kind of finish, say tiles or slate, I certainly would have poured it as soon as possible.

Making Headers and Posts

Once we had a platform to work on, we made a cut table and mounted the cut-off saw on it. If you build a steel-frame house, I strongly suggest you do the same. Instead of taking the saw to the woodpile, you bring the steel to the cut table.

Posts are made up of two studs and two lengths of track. All our posts were made of

Tips from a Veteran Steel Builder

During my 16 years in the building business, I've worked as designer and inspector on jobs that ranged from office buildings to a wind tunnel for NASA. That experience prepared me well for my current career, which is designing and supervising the assembly of steel houses on the Olympic Peninsula in Washington State. In the past three years, I've detailed plans for more than 50 houses and been the general contractor for a half-dozen homes.

I like framing with light-gauge steel because for about the same price as wood, you end up with a more structurally sound, termite-proof, rot-proof, rodent-resistant, straight, and true structure. What's more, instead of burning waste or paying to dump it, you can recycle nearly all the leftovers. But working with steel, you must be fastidious at every stage of construction. If you just slap a house together, steel framing will be your worst nightmare. I strongly suggest that builders who are new to steel but familiar with wood construction hire an experienced steel framer to work alongside the crew during its first steel project.

Buy Extra, and Start Out Dead Level

We order approximately 90% of our steel to be delivered cut to length. Track (wall plates) is best ordered in standard 10-ft. lengths. I always order at least 10% more track, and 50 to 100 extra structural wall studs. We use standard stud lengths just as in wood framing, but with steel the studs are 97 in. long. I keep a small stock of the most common studs and joists so that I always have a few extra available. I find that a magnetic level (at least 4 ft. long) is essential, and a 50-ft.- to 100-ft.-long water level helps immensely in leveling the top plates of the walls.

A flat, level foundation is critical when framing with steel. We make that condition clear to our concrete subs, and we retire and rehire them accordingly.

When the steel is delivered to the site, we lay out the components in an orderly fashion. First we assemble all the headers and beams required to erect the first floor, and we pack them full of fiberglass insulation. Then we lay out the bottom tracks that are to be connected directly to the concrete foundation. We put these tracks atop a ⅛-in.-thick, 6-in.-wide strip of polystyrene sill sealer. This step prevents electrolysis between the concrete and the steel. At this point we roll out the floor joists and sheathe the floor with plywood. We use #6 Grabber brand self-drilling bugle-head screws to affix the plywood, along with construction adhesive glue.

We lay out all our studs 24 in. o. c., and we frame and sheathe our walls while they are lying on the subfloor or slab. We check every bottom-to-top track dimension at each stud as we assemble the wall, and we clamp a long floor joist to the bottom track to keep it straight as we assemble the wall. Then we check the wall for squareness.

At this point only the two end studs are screwed to their tracks. All others are being held with Vise-Grip clamps. After the wall is squared, we screw off the 20-ga. material. The studs are placed vertically, with their legs pointing at one another, in the bottom track of the wall. The distance between the studs is equal to the inside dimension of the track that will unite them. I found it easier to install the top track of the wall, and then come back and screw the tracks onto the studs to complete the posts (see the photo on p. 27). Before screwing the tracks onto their studs, stuff the post with insulation. You can't do it after the pieces are assembled.

A header is made the same way as a post, but it's easier to build the header on the ground and then lift it into place rather than to try to build the thing in the wall. The headers we made were 10 in. by 3⅝ in. They are remarkably strong. Because of the strength of the steel, Berle designed a number of corner windows that required no center posts. The roof loads are carried by impressively cantilevered headers.

rest of the connections and sheathe the wall with ½-in. CDX plywood. The plywood sheeting provides shear value as well as acts as a thermal barrier. The wall is now ready to stand and be temporarily braced. We do not screw off the interior-side connections until all the bearing walls are completed and in place. This step allows us to fine-tune alignment and height of all the walls all at once, minimizing our top-plate height variations while maintaining our ⅛-in. allowable tolerance.

We have framed roofs both with site-built steel trusses and with factory-built wood trusses. And we've learned that complicated roofs, low-pitch roofs, and most hip roofs can be built with wood for less cost than steel. Because wood-truss assemblies are standardized and are factory built, they are less expensive to buy and take less labor to install. But if you want the advantages of steel framing, almost all roofs can be framed with steel if you have the time and the budget.

Use Commercial Subs; They're Used to Steel

Here on the Olympic Peninsula, there are quite a few commercial contractors willing to work on steel-framed residential projects. So we have found it fairly easy to find plumbers, electricians, and mechanical contractors who are willing and able to do our projects at a competitive price.

Insulating steel-frame homes is no big deal. I advise our clients to use the Blow-In Blanket® System from Ark-Seal. It's a fiberglass insulation blown into wall cavities, filling voids in studs, around wiring and electrical boxes, and around plumbing. The fibers are laced with a glue that holds the insulation in place, preventing settling. Installers use hot glue to stick nylon mesh to the studs. The nozzle that delivers the insulation is then poked through small holes cut in the mesh.

We don't use a plastic vapor retarder between the studs and the drywall. Instead, we finish the drywall with vapor-barrier paint, which limits the transfer of moisture through the walls. If you choose a plastic vapor retarder, however, you can adhere the plastic to the studs with hot glue.

If you want to get your feet wet without risking much, try using steel studs for your interior nonbearing walls. Steel studs will save you money on material costs, and they will give your framers a chance to get used to the material.

Designers can learn more about detailing steel houses by contacting the American Iron and Steel Institute. Ask for their handbook RG-930, *Residential Steel Framing Manual for Architects, Engineers and Builders* ($40). Finally, steel manufacturers all have span tables and engineering-specification books free for the asking. You should be aware that some steel manufacturers' span tables assume that you are using web stiffeners at ends and at centers of joist spans, and some span tables don't.

Steven Jacobs is vice president of Cottage Steel Industries in Port Orchard, Washington.

The Rafters Don't Need Bird's Mouths

Unlike most wood rafters, a metal rafter doesn't require a bird's mouth because the rafters are held in place atop the wall by a metal angle clip. The angle clip is placed directly over a double stud or post and then screwed to the side of the rafter so that the rafter's load is transferred down through the clip.

Our rafters were attached to our ridge beam with the same type of angle clip. Because of this connection, it was only necessary to cut our rafters to within ¼ in. of the ridge beam. There was no need for an exact measurement between the wall plate and the ridge beam, so this portion of the project went quickly. At the eave line, a track that's screwed to the ends of the rafters acts as blocking.

The spacing of our rafters is irregular, so to gain a consistent layout for the plywood

decking, we screwed purlins made of 20-ga. hat channel to the rafters (see the photo above) at 24 in. o. c. The purlins provide support for sheathing and create a ventilation channel above the insulation.

Wood Sheathing and Nailers for Shingles and Windows

Even though the skeleton of this house is steel right down to the foundation, we still found it convenient to skin it with plywood for the roof deck and for the shingled exterior walls. We used #8, 1-in. self-tapping pan-head screws to affix the plywood decking to the 20-ga. purlins. We used self-tapping screws instead of self-drilling screws on the roof deck because it's easier to get force behind the drill when you're pushing down on it.

We used our nail guns to affix the plywood wall sheathing to 2x4 nailers. Attaching the nailers to the steel studs gave us a chance to use yet another kind of specialized screw: a self-drilling screw with wings (see the bottom photo on p. 30). This screw has a pair of cutters above its self-tapping tip that bore a hole in the wood larger than the diameter of the threaded shank. This larger

hole keeps the threads from engaging the 2x4 when the screw spins without penetrating the metal as the tip cuts a hole in the stud. With an ordinary self-drilling screw, the 2x4 climbs the shank as the screw spins. Once the stud is penetrated, the wings break, and the threads drive into the metal.

A Magnetic Drill Press Helps with the Big Holes

In some places, we were able to reduce the number of screws required by using larger fasteners. For example, the plans called for ¼-in. self-drilling screws to tie the 16-ga. X-braces to the steel-plate hold-downs. The hold-downs were ¼ in. thick—too much to expect a self-drilling screw to penetrate. Because we had to predrill the holes anyway, we talked it over with the engineer and redesigned the hold-down using ½-in. machine bolts. But how could we drill the holes efficiently? The answer turned out to be a Milwaukee® Electromagnetic Portable Drill Press (see the photo below), which we rented for the occasion. Flip the switch, and

This drill is self-supporting. An electromagnetic drill press clamps onto a workpiece. Here the author drills ½-in. holes in a ¼-in. steel hold-down and a 16-ga. diagonal strap.

the baseplate on this baby grabs hold of the workpiece with the grip of death. Using this tool made it quick and easy to drill the 110 holes for the braces.

Casings, Drywall, and Baseboards

Unlike the windows, the door openings weren't wrapped with wood. Instead, I screwed a track onto the studs on each side of a door opening, and then screwed the jambs of our prehung doors to the tracks. I used yet another kind of screw in this instance—a square-drive trim screw with a self-drilling point (see the middle photo on p. 30). I used these screws because they don't leave much of a hole in the jamb to fill. But the jambs will climb right up the shanks of these screws if you don't clamp the jambs to the studs.

There is some debate among designers and builders about condensation in the walls of houses that are framed with metal studs. Some folks believe that warm, moist interior air might go from a vapor to a liquid on the steel frame under certain conditions.

We decided to install a 6-mil poly vapor barrier on the inside of the frame. This became a hassle. You can't just hammer-tack the stuff to the studs and joists. Instead, we tried getting it to stick by coating the studs with 3M® spray adhesive. That didn't work. Both the studs and the plastic were too slippery. So we put duct-tape patches on the plastic over the studs and ran pan-head screws through them. This had to be one of the most frustrating parts of the project. My guess is that the airtight drywall approach, which uses foam gaskets behind drywall coated with vapor-barrier paint, is a better way to solve this problem.

My advice is to leave the hanging of the drywall to the professionals who have commercial experience. If you decide to hang your own drywall, be sure to use bugle-head screws with self-drilling points. A standard, pointed-tip drywall screw will penetrate a 20-ga. stud, but we learned that by the time the screw goes into the stud, the spinning screw has excavated a hole in the drywall that is larger than the head of the screw. We trimmed the bottoms of the walls with MDF baseboards. We used the square-drive self-drilling trim screws to attach them, along with a continuous bead of construction adhesive.

So How Do You Like Working with Steel?

Faster assembly is one of the advantages of steel construction that turns up in most of the articles and brochures on the subject. That may be true for a simple house, but in my experience it just isn't so for a complicated custom house. The labor cost was double what we thought it was going to be.

The cost of the steel, however, was a lot less than the materials would have cost for the house to be framed of wood. All the steel, plus the fasteners required to assemble the frame, cost about $17,000 for this 1,800 sq. ft. house. The same parts in wood penciled out at about $40,000. That's a pretty impressive difference. I easily could build a simple house of steel, knowing what I know now, for less than a comparable house of wood.

For me, though, building with steel just isn't much fun. I think part of the problem is that it takes so long to fasten the frame together. When I think back on this job, one thing really sticks out in my mind: There was never a time when the job took off. With wood construction, there are times when changes come slowly, but then there are sweeping changes when the walls are lifted into place and the sheathing goes on. Steel construction just seems to plod along. I expect all that will change when somebody comes up with the steel-framing equivalent of the nail gun.

Cost estimates are from 1995.

Robert McCullough *is a custom builder living in Seattle, Washington.*

Sources

American Iron and Steel Institute
1140 Connecticut Ave. Ste. 705
Washington, D.C. 20036
(202) 452-7100
www.steel.org

Ark-Seal
2185 S. Jason St.
Denver, CO 80223
(800) 525-8992
www.arkseal.com

Norton Co.
1 New Bond St.
Worcester, MA 01606
(800) 543-4335

Simple Tools for Faster Framing

■ BY LARRY HAUN

When I was a child, long western-Nebraska winters kept me inside and close to the kitchen stove. In the 1930s, with no television and no department stores, there wasn't much to do except help my mother sew. It was then that I learned to make patterns and templates.

Some years later, when we built the roof on the first house I worked on, the master carpenter laid out and cut a full-length common rafter that became the pattern. Its outline was marked, one board at a time, on a pile of 2x rafter stock. As with my mother's clothing patterns, the hardest part was making the first one.

In this article, I'll describe some devices, patterns, templates, and tools that I've used to make repetitive work easier. Some you might have seen before, some not. Either way, these examples might spark your own ingenuity. On any decent-size framing job, it's productive to make a template. A simple tool takes a few minutes to make, but it'll save you time in the long run.

Mark Anchor-Bolt Locations with a Simple Steel Tool

When framing on a concrete slab or foundation, I mark locations of anchor-bolt holes in the sill with a bolt-hole marker. These markers are available commercially from Pairis Enterprises, but are easy to make (see the illustration at right).

To use the bolt marker, place the mudsill plate on the foundation with the edge of the sill temporarily on the opposite side of the chalkline from where it normally would go. Check to make sure the plate is positioned directly on the line and that the end of the plate is in the right spot. Hold the notch in the bolt marker against the anchor bolt and perpendicular to the plate. Tap the screw or bolt in the tool with a hammer to leave an indentation on the sill, marking the location to be drilled. Drill the holes and drop the mudsill over the bolts. The mudsill should fall in place right on the line.

Layout Stick Quickly Marks Stud Location

The layout stick has been around as a simple framing tool for over 60 years. It's used to lay out the locations of studs (see the photo at right). Mine was made of aluminum, but you can make a good one from wood. Cut a strip of ¾-in. plywood or 1x stock 1½ in. wide and 49½ in. long. (That's the dimension, outside to outside, of four studs 16 in. o. c., and this length seems to be the most manageable.) To this stick, attach strips of plywood 1½ in. wide and 9½ in. long at 16 in. o. c., or whatever spacing the layout calls for. Let the strips overhang 3 in. on one side and 5 in. on the other. The 3-in. legs allow you to mark stud locations on the edges of top and bottom plates at the same time. The 5-in. legs make it easy to mark two plates laid side by side or two plates and a header at the same time.

Locate Anchor-bolt Holes Quickly with a Bolt Marker

Place the notched end of the tool against the anchor bolt. Then tap the stove bolt with a hammer to leave an indentation in the mudsill plate, marking the anchor-bolt site.

18-in. plate strap

Slight bend makes marker easier to use.

Lag screw or stove bolt

Notch

Chalklines

3½ in. for a 2x4 plate

2x4 mudsill plate

Concrete slab

Anchor bolt

A homemade template speeds stud layout. Using a layout stick to mark stud locations can be faster than measuring 16-in. increments with a tape. Metal layout sticks will last longer, but scrap plywood works fine in a pinch.

With a corner and channel marker, you can quickly transfer the location of an intersecting wall to both the face and edges of top and bottom wall plates.

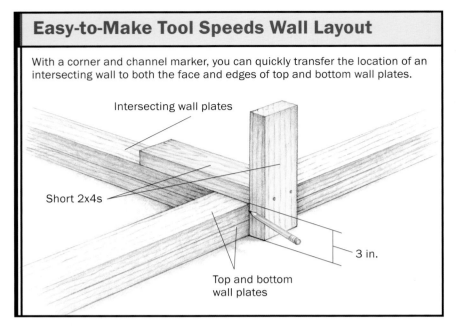

Intersecting wall plates

Short 2x4s

3 in.

Top and bottom wall plates

Drilling guide locates bolt holes. A simple template makes fast work of drilling holes for hold-down brackets.

Corner and Channel Marker

When you're laying out stacked top and bottom plates, the location of studs at intersecting walls, which form a channel, can be marked rapidly on the plates with a corner and channel marker (see the illustration above). You can nail a wooden one together in about a minute.

Place this tool on the plate where one wall intersects another, and mark both bottom and top plates on all edges and on the face of the top plate. These lines show where to locate backing studs for drywall and where to cut the second top plate so that the walls can interlock.

Installing Hold-Downs

Hold-downs are metal brackets bolted to the foundation and to 4x posts in wall framing (see the photo above). Hold-downs help keep a house stable and tied to its foundation in an earthquake or in high-wind country. When a job has multiple hold-downs, I make a small L-shaped template from plywood or 1x stock. The holes in the template match the holes in the hold-down. The template acts as a guide for drilling the posts.

Cut Blocking Quickly on a Graduated Bench

When a radial-arm or sliding miter saw is not available, blocking can be cut rapidly with a circular saw. First, nail an 8-ft. or 10-ft. length of 2x to a windowsill or to a wall stud, about 3 ft. off the floor (see the top photo on the facing page). Prop up the other end with a 2x leg. Starting at the wall and moving out, make a series of lines, 14½ in. apart, for instance, across the face of the bench. Place a piece of stock, long or short, on this 2x, and make a cut at every mark. Remember that blocks usually don't have to be cut with great precision. If one block is a hair short, the next will be a bit long, and they will all average out.

New Life for an Old Level

There are a lot of fancy levels on the market today. My experience with a good level is that it doesn't stay good for long on most framing jobs. I learned early on how to take

Cutting blocking is quicker with a graduated bench. One method the author uses to cut blocking is to build a simple bench from dimension lumber, supporting one end from an interior partition wall and propping up the other. The blocking is cut by siting along marks made across the bench every 14½ in.

a battered 2-ft. level and make it into an accurate plumb stick (see the photo at right).

Nail two pieces of 1x2, about 16 in. long, to the edge of a straight, lightweight stud, one piece on each end. Let the sticks overhang the stud ends 3 in. or 4 in. Overhanging allows the plumb stick to rest against the top and bottom plates and not against a bowed stud that could produce an inaccurate reading. Attach the level to the opposite edge of the stud with duct tape or heavy rubber bands, high enough so that the bubble in the vial will be at eye level.

To check the plumb stick for accuracy, hold it upright with the face of the stud flat against the wall and the 1x extensions touching the bottom and top plates. Move the top of the stick back and forth until the bubble is centered exactly in the vial, and mark along the 1x extensions. Now turn the plumb stick around so that the opposite face of the stud is flat against the wall, and line the extensions up with the marks on the plates. If the bubble returns to the exact center of the vial, the plumb stick is accurate.

Fix an inaccurate level with a plumb stick. To check a plumb stick for accuracy, mark the stick's location against the top and bottom plates. Then flip the stick around and put it back on the marks. If the level is off, correct it with a shim between the level and the stick.

If the bubble is not centered in the vial, the level needs to be adjusted. Stick a wooden shim, a folded piece of paper or even an 8d nail under one end of the level and check the plumb stick again. Keep adjusting the shim until the bubble is centered both ways.

Gain leverage with a push stick. To plumb a newly framed wall, cut a 1x4 or 1x6 about 2 ft. longer than the wall studs. Wedge the top of the stick against the top plate, then bend it by pushing down and holding it in place with your foot. As you pull up on the stick, the wall will move.

Move Walls with a Push Stick

When plumbing and lining a house frame, I like to use what I call a push stick to rack walls end to end and make them plumb (see the photo above). Pick out a knot-free 1x4 or 1x6 and cut it about 2 ft. longer than the height of the wall you're working on. Place the upper end of the stick under the top plate, against a stud. To gain the most leverage, the stick needs to be as close to parallel with the wall as possible. Bend the stick down, holding the bottom end against the floor with one foot. Now pull the middle of the stick up. As the board straightens, the wall will move.

Rafter-Cutting Templates

If you've read my articles on roof framing, you know I use rafter templates to scribe the ridge plumb-cut line and the bird's mouth cutlines on rafters (see the top illustration on the facing page). Using a rafter template is much faster than using a full-length rafter as a pattern.

To make a template, start with a 2-ft.-long piece of plywood or 1x stock the same width as the rafters. I use a small triangle square to mark the template, but you can do the same with a framing square.

Use the square to mark the ridge plumb-cut line at one end of the template and the level- and plumb-cut lines of the bird's mouth at the other end. Cut along these lines, and then nail a 1x2 fence to the upper edge of the template. The fence lets you place the template on the rafter and transfer the marks rapidly and accurately.

If you load all of the rafter stock on edge on wide, sturdy rafter horses, you can then use the template to mark the ridge plumb-cut line quickly on each rafter, sliding the boards out of the way as you go.

To mark the bird's-mouth cuts, keep the rafter stock lined up and on edge. Instead of using a tape measure to mark each rafter individually, mark the length of only the first and last rafters in the rack. Then, with a chalkline, snap a line across the rest of the rafters. With the chalkline as a reference, use the template to mark each bird's mouth.

Rafter Templates Are Light and Quick

To use a rafter template, first line up all of the stock on rafter horses. Measure and mark the length of the first and last rafters in the rack. Snap a chalkline across the rest of the rafters and then use the pattern to mark the plumb-cut and level-cut lines on each rafter.

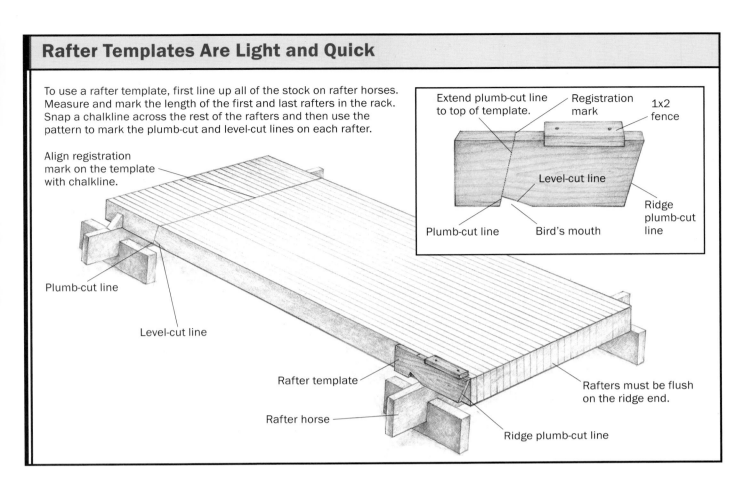

Align registration mark on the template with chalkline.

Plumb-cut line

Level-cut line

Rafter template

Rafter horse

Ridge plumb-cut line

Rafters must be flush on the ridge end.

Extend plumb-cut line to top of template.

Registration mark

1x2 fence

Level-cut line

Plumb-cut line

Bird's mouth

Ridge plumb-cut line

A Simple Platform Helps to Get Plywood to the Roof

When I don't have a forklift to raise sheathing to the roof, I build a staging platform out of 2x4s (see illustration at right). Nail two studs on edge into the wall framing about 3 ft. apart, extending out from the building about 5 ft. Support the studs with legs that reach the ground. Place sheets of plywood on the studs and tip them up so that they rest against the rafter tails or fascia board. Now all you have to do is reach down from the roof, grab a sheet, and pull it up.

On two-story houses, sometimes you can build a platform on a balcony and then move the sheathing up in stages.

Larry Haun is the author of Habitat for Humanity: How to Build a House (2002), published by The Taunton Press, Inc. He lives in Coos Bay, Oregon.

Platform Holds Plywood near the Roof

To help get sheathing to the roof, build a 2x4 staging platform. Nail two 2x4s into the wall framing about 3 ft. apart, supporting the ends with legs that reach the ground.

Sheathing

2x4s nailed to wall framing

Sources

Pairis Enterprises
27574 Commerce
Center Dr.
Unit 133
Temecula, CA 92590
(909) 676-3038

Framing Corners

■ BY CHARLES BICKFORD

Unless you are a builder who always builds round houses, chances are pretty good that a portion of your building career will be spent framing corners. Until recently, framing a corner was a straightforward task that didn't present too many options. The typical stick-framed corner was, like its predecessor the timber post, a massive piece of wood. It was sturdy, and you could drive nails into it anywhere you pleased. These days, the traditional three-stud corner is not gone but may soon become as rare as solid-chestnut timbers. For a variety of reasons, there is now more to consider than just providing nailing support for siding outside and drywall inside.

The primary reason is economics. The price of framing lumber has nearly doubled in the past 10 years. The prevailing opinion holds that the lumber's quality has slipped considerably, too, which is an economic factor if you have to spend 20 minutes digging in the pile trying to find a straight 2x for a sill or a plate. The cost of heating a house has also changed the way people frame cor-

ners. During the energy crunch of the 1970s, some architects and builders began to think harder about more efficient ways to insulate houses and switched from 2x4 to 2x6 walls for their greater R-value potential. Corners, always notorious cold spots, came under scrutiny, too. If built with 2x6s, the older-style solid corners not only required more lumber than the 2x4 version, but they also created a bigger area in the wall that couldn't be insulated and suffered more from thermal bridging. Thermal bridging is the transfer of heat energy through solid materials; in a house, cold is usually conducted from the outside sheathing to the interior walls through any solid material, most notably the framing.

In the interest of both economy and energy efficiency, researchers and builders have been searching for better ways of framing corners using less wood and more insulation. Here are some of the methods that they've come up with.

Charles Bickford is Senior Editor at Fine Home-building.

Three-Stud Corner

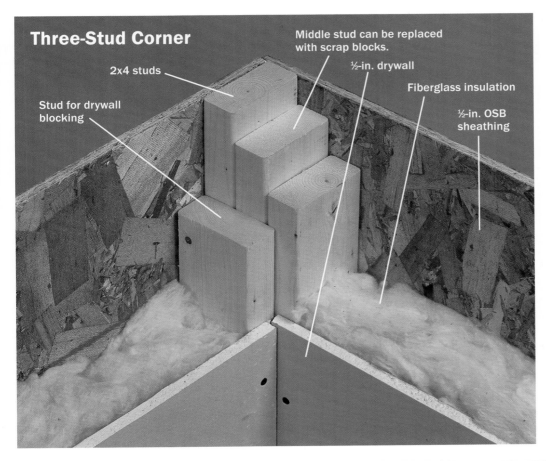

2x4 studs

Stud for drywall blocking

Middle stud can be replaced with scrap blocks.

½-in. drywall

Fiberglass insulation

½-in. OSB sheathing

The three-stud corner (see the photo at left) is a direct descendant of the timber post and is favored by many builders. Its main advantages are that it is quick to assemble, it is strong and it gives the carpenter plenty of support for nailing exterior corner boards and siding. You can make it two ways: Nail three full studs together, or use 2x scrap from the site as blocks between two full studs. A single end stud on the abutting wall is nailed on the inside corner. The main disadvantages of three-stud corners are that they use more lumber, are difficult to insulate, and create a wide thermal bridge to the interior. These corners are not effective when built with 2x6s. Connecticut framer Mario Sapia uses this corner because he likes the mass of the construction; he reduces the thermal bridging by wrapping the exterior of the house in ¾-in. rigid-foam insulation.

The two-stud corner (see the photo at right), also known as the California corner, is popular with builders because it goes together quickly and because it uses less lumber. It is also more energy efficient because it has less mass to create a thermal bridge and opens a larger space that's easy to insulate. Some builders don't use it because the corner gives them less to nail to if they're putting up vinyl siding or corner boards. Veteran California framer Don Dunkley likes to use the two-stud configuration for interior corners but wants beefier corners on exterior walls that will hold the strapping and bolts necessary to comply with earthquake regulations. The two-stud corner works equally well in 2x4 and 2x6 walls.

Two-Stud Corner

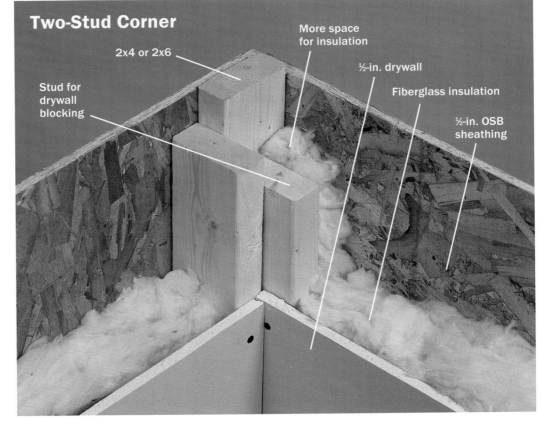

2x4 or 2x6

Stud for drywall blocking

More space for insulation

½-in. drywall

Fiberglass insulation

½-in. OSB sheathing

One-Stud Corner with Clips

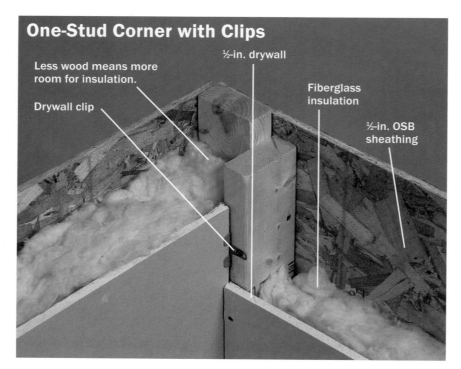

Less wood means more room for insulation.

Drywall clip

½-in. drywall

Fiberglass insulation

½-in. OSB sheathing

A variation on the two-stud corner, the one-stud corner is a direct result of the switch from drywall nails to drywall screws. The hammer-proof 2x nailers in corners can be replaced with a thinner nailer (see the middle photo at left) or with drywall clips (see the photos at left and below) because screws need less backing support than nails. By nailing a 1x3 or a 3-in. wide strip of plywood to the inside corner, you eliminate an additional stud, thereby saving wood and creating room for insulation. Drywall clips (see the sidebar on the facing page) eliminate the need for wood nailers and further increase the available wall-cavity space for insulation. Instead of clips, Bill Eich of Spirit Lake, Iowa, has long strips of light-gauge steel bent lengthwise at right angles (resembling drywall corner bead), measuring approximately 1½ in. per side. His carpenters then screw the strips to the appropriate studs, where the strips serve as cheap, efficient drywall backers.

One-Stud Corner with Nailer

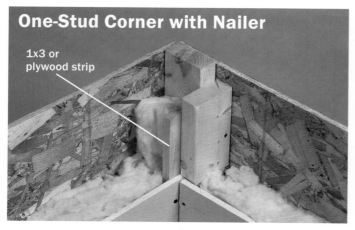

1x3 or plywood strip

One-Stud Corner with Light-Gauge Steel Backer

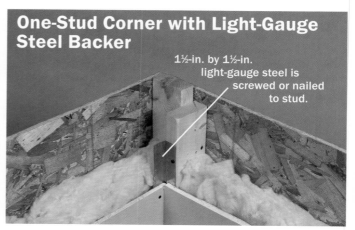

1½-in. by 1½-in. light-gauge steel is screwed or nailed to stud.

Nonthermal Bridging Corner

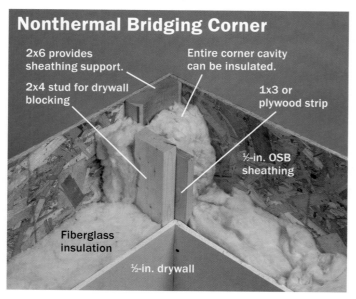

2x6 provides sheathing support.

2x4 stud for drywall blocking

Entire corner cavity can be insulated.

1x3 or plywood strip

½-in. OSB sheathing

Fiberglass insulation

½-in. drywall

Contributing editor Mike Guertin has long been concerned with exterior corners, which can be notorious cold cavities. Although thermal bridging is a concern along the entire wall, framing alternatives such as double-stud walls are not cost-effective. Corners, on the other hand, carry less load than a typical stud and are structurally more flexible. Guertin is experimenting with a 2x6 corner (see the photo at left) that can be completely insulated. He uses a 2x6 on the exterior corner and nails a 2x4 and a 1x3, or a strip of plywood, together to form the interior corner. He can now insulate throughout the corner cavity, eliminating thermal bridging by breaking contact between the outer sheathing and the drywall. Guertin says that the corner still provides good support for top plates and for nailing. (Although Guertin's building inspector approved the corner, check with your local inspector before trying it.)

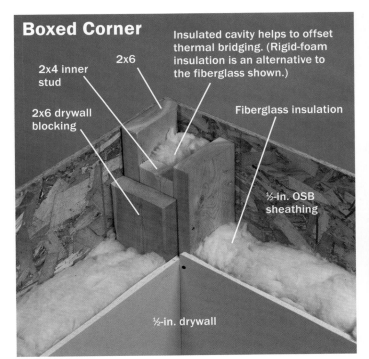

Boxed Corner

2x4 inner stud

2x6

2x6 drywall blocking

Insulated cavity helps to offset thermal bridging. (Rigid-foam insulation is an alternative to the fiberglass shown.)

Fiberglass insulation

½-in. OSB sheathing

½-in. drywall

Here's another corner that is fairly popular (see the photo at left). Typically used in a 2x6 wall, the outer studs used are 2x6s, while the inner stud can be a 2x4. John Carroll, a builder from North Carolina, uses a variation on this theme when nailing wider corner boards but uses another 2x6 in place of the 2x4. In both examples, framers should have insulation ready on site because the interior of the box must be insulated before the sheathing is nailed to offset the potential of thermal bridging.

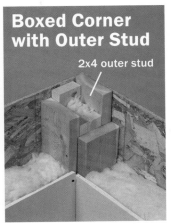

Boxed Corner with Outer Stud

2x4 outer stud

Builders who require more nailing for corner boards will sometimes put an additional stud on the outside of the box after insulating its interior (see the photo at left).

Drywall Clips: Engineered Hardware That Takes the Place of Wood

Carpenters and wood are as inseparable as bakers and flour. But unlike wheat, trees cannot be harvested on an annual schedule, and we all know that lumber is not as plentiful, cheap, or straight as it used to be. One way to slow the drain on your wallet and on lumber supplies is to use drywall clips.

Clips are used in place of wood backing to support drywall in corners (walls and ceilings). Depending on the style, drywall clips are slipped on to the drywall or nailed to the stud and can be installed either by the framers or by the drywall crews. All clips are usually installed 16 in. o. c. to support the first sheet of drywall in the corner; any

protruding tabs are covered by the succeeding sheet. Because the clips take the place of a stud in a corner, there is also greater space in the wall cavity to fill with insulation.

The clips certainly are not mainstream items, even though they've been on the market in some form for more than two decades. Contractors familiar with the product say that the clips offer a sturdy and economic alternative to lumber. The clips run from 12¢ to about 20¢ each. These clips may be hard to find at the lumberyard, so check the Yellow Pages under "Drywall Supplies" or contact manufacturers.

DS Drywall Stop (light-gauge steel)

The Nailer (recycled HDPE)

Corner-Back Fasteners (light-gauge steel)

Three-Stud Intersection

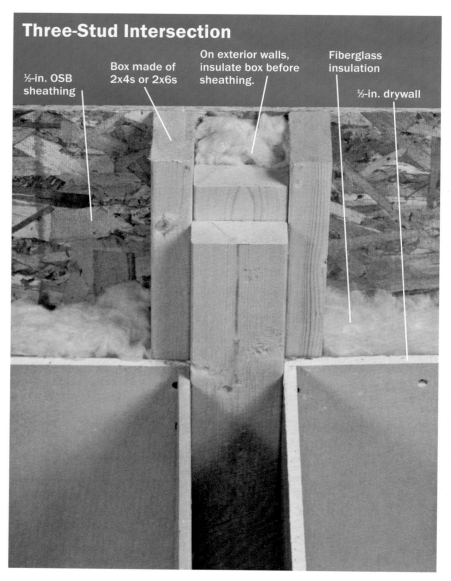

½-in. OSB sheathing

Box made of 2x4s or 2x6s

On exterior walls, insulate box before sheathing.

Fiberglass insulation

½-in. drywall

A traditional method of building T-intersections is nailing the intersecting wall to a box, sometimes called a channel, built into the adjacent wall (see the photo at left). To lessen thermal loss (if the adjacent wall is an exterior wall), this box must also be insulated before the exterior is sheathed. Blocks nailed horizontally between studs (see the photo below) in the adjacent wall are a second method of forming the corner and a good place to use scrap lumber; the intersecting wall is then nailed to the blocks. Some builders prefer a faster third method (see the photo at bottom left) and nail a wider (a 2x6 on a 2x4 wall, for instance) piece of stock on the flat that provides nailing for both the intersecting wall and the drywall in one shot. When the framing, insulation, and drywall crews are working in close synch, it's also possible to drywall the entire first wall and then nail the new wall through the gypsum into the nailer. This method creates fewer breaks in the vapor barrier. Drywall clips do the work in the fourth method (see the photo at bottom right).

T-Intersection with Nailer

Larger 2x nailer (2x6 shown)

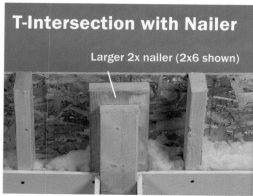

T-Intersection with Blocking

Horizontal 2x blocking

Continuous drywall behind intersection makes a tighter envelope.

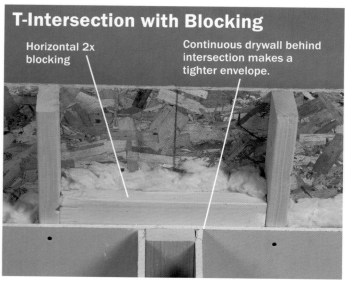

T-Intersection with Clips

Drywall clips take the place of wood blocking.

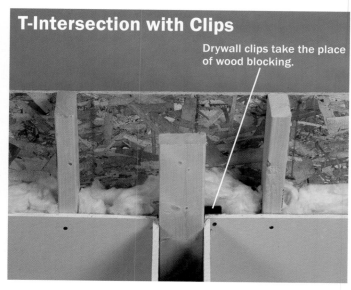

Corners greater than 90° present problems of their own. In the conventional method, studs aligned with their respective plates meet in a splayed fashion and are sometimes difficult to nail together into a straight corner. (Crooked corners can give drywall contractors fits.) Contributing editor Scott McBride uses a sturdier method (see the photo at right). With a table saw or a circular saw, he rips a 4x4 in half at 22½°, flips one half around and nails the two halves together. If there are a fair number of these corners on a job, Don Dunkley will rip 2x4s at a 45° angle and nail the long blocks into the widest part of the cavity (see the photo below). This not only makes a larger nailing surface but also allows for insulation.

Solid Oblique Corner

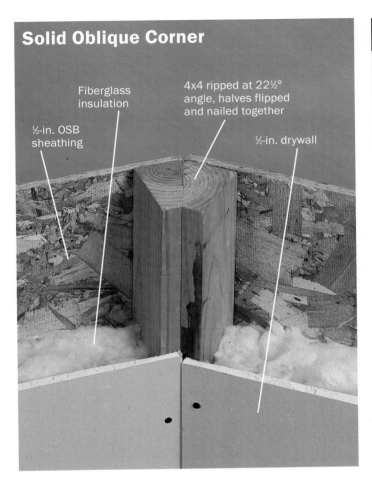

Fiberglass insulation

4x4 ripped at 22½° angle, halves flipped and nailed together

½-in. OSB sheathing

½-in. drywall

Sources

Here is a partial listing of drywall-clip manufacturers. It is by no means inclusive.

DRYWALL STOP
Simpson Strong-Tie Co.
4637 Chabot Drive, #200
Pleasanton, CA 94588
(800) 999-5099
http://www.strongtie.com
DS Drywall Stop (light-gauge steel)

THE NAILER
The Millennium Group
2300 W. Eisenhower Blvd.
Loveland, CO 80537
(800) 280-2304
www.thenailer.com
The Nailer

PREST-ON CLIPS
Prest-on Co.
312 Lookout Point
Hot Springs, AR 71901
(888) 323-1813
www.prest-on.com
Corner-Back fasteners (light-gauge steel)

Blocked Oblique Corner

2x4 studs

A 2x block ripped at 45° and nailed into studs stabilizes the corner and prevents spreading.

Fiberglass insulation

½-in. OSB sheathing

½-in. drywall

Framing and Sheathing Floors

■ BY RICK ARNOLD AND MIKE GUERTIN

We've finished backfilling the foundation, and the mudsills are level and square. Now the real fun begins: saws screaming, hammers humming, sawdust flying. But as anxious as we are to shift into high-gear production mode, we always approach the task of floor framing methodically and thoughtfully. With this strategy, everything goes together right the first time, and the reciprocating saw and the cat's paw stay in the toolbox where they belong.

A Good Framing Plan Streamlines Layout and Installation

Before we even think about getting our tools out, and usually before breaking ground, we start our floor on paper with a framing plan (see the illustration on p. 52). Most of the house plans we work from do not include a framing layout, so usually we create our own.

First, we choose the best starting point for the joist layout to minimize the number of joists and the subfloor waste. After looking at how the house is laid out (where the jogs are; how the roof trusses will be laid out; where bearing walls are; where toilets, tubs, and showers fall), we decide where to begin the layout. With the house featured in this article, the natural starting point was the front left corner because of the two adjoining sections where the joists changed direction. When in doubt, we usually pick the 90° corner that has the longest uninterrupted legs. All smaller sections are then blended into the larger layout.

On our plans we draw lines for each joist, header, in-floor beam, and any special framing details for the house. By using a different colored pencil for each joist length, we can use the plan for accurate material ordering later. When materials are delivered, the joist plan also enables us to direct the different-

With careful layout and by precutting all the joists, framing a floor is like fitting together a giant jigsaw puzzle.

The Best Floor Layout Begins on Paper

Before any lumber is ordered, a detailed framing plan should be drawn. The framing plan exposes potential problem areas such as bearing walls and plumbing, or floor openings that might require special attention, and the color code (inset) indicates joist lengths for ordering and then precutting lumber when it arrives.

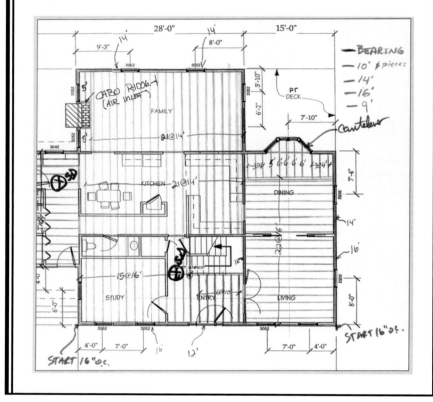

The big exception to that rule is where the house has bearing walls running parallel to the floor joists. In those cases we usually double or triple joists under the bearing wall to carry the weight. However, if a plumber or HVAC sub plans to use a bearing wall for drains or ducts, we identify the exact location of the wall on our plan and place the joists under the outside edges of the wall. Solid blocking is then installed between the joists every 2 ft. or so, leaving space for the systems to come through. We also double the joists beneath large tubs or whirlpools if the fixture is to sit in the middle of the joist span.

Floor Details Are Spelled Out in the Layout

Once the foundation is poured and back-filled, we take great care installing and adjusting mudsills (see "Squaring and Leveling Mudsills," pp. 12–21), carrying beams, and basement bearing walls. As we prepare for the floor, everything is kept level and square, and the dimensions on the plans are matched exactly. The closer that we keep the tolerances at the floor-deck stage, the quicker and easier the rest of the house framing will proceed. Before beginning our layout, we string the carrying beams and bearing walls and brace them to keep them straight. These strings are left in place so that we can double-check the walls again after the joists are installed.

To ensure consistency, one crew member does all the joist layout. We begin our layout by marking any special features of the floor deck that interrupt common joist layout. In addition to the chimney and stair openings, the project featured in this article had a cantilevered section, in-floor beams, and two areas where the joists change direction.

These special details and measurements are marked with a lumber crayon on the sill plates to alert the crew that the standard lay-

length 2xs to the appropriate areas of the floor with just a glance.

We try to have a preliminary meeting (or at least a couple of quick faxes) with the plumber and heating contractor to identify any joists that might pose a problem with their systems. We can also alert each contractor if we see that both of them expect to fill the same joist bay. By moving a joist a couple of inches to one side or to the other, we sometimes can resolve competition for space. We generally try to avoid having a joist positioned directly below a wall above, and knowing which interior walls will contain vents, drains, or ductwork keeps us from placing a joist where it might have to be cut.

out has changed. Someone following the layout person can then precut the odd pieces, and the installation is easy and obvious. By the way, if an opening in the floor happens to cross a carrying beam, we snap lines across the beam from the marks on the opposite sill plates to keep our measurements consistent.

Make Sure the "X" Is on the Right Side of Line

With all the special features of the deck laid out, the next step is laying out the common joists on the sill plates that run perpendicular to the joists. This floor called for 2x10 floor joists laid out on 16-in. centers.

String keeps the layout uniform. The blue string in the foreground was stretched between the layout marks on the sills. Measurements on the carrying beams are then taken from that line.

Starting from the end we determined on our plan, we make marks ¾ in. shy of each 16-in. symbol on the measuring tape. When the entire sill plate or beam is marked off, we go back and make a square line at each mark and draw an X forward of each line. The same procedure is repeated on the opposite side of the house starting at the same end.

Next, we run a line between our starting marks on the sill plates across any intermediate bearing walls or beams. This line gives us a reference point from which to lay out the tops of the bearing walls or the carrying beams (see the photo at left). The uniform starting point helps to keep the joists in a straight line and makes it easy to lay down the subflooring later. Walls and beams are then measured and marked at 16-in. intervals from that point.

The main body of the floor featured in this article is 44 ft. deep. The span is broken into two 14-ft. sections and one 16-ft. section. The joists in the front section will be set ahead of our marks as indicated by the Xs. The middle section will be set behind the mark, and the rear section will be set ahead of the mark like the front. The two outside sill plates get only one line to indicate the location for each joist. But on the two internal beams where joists from adjoining sections will overlap, we add additional lines indicating the outside edges of the joists. (Because we toenail the overlapping joists to the beam after both joists are in place, a single layout line would be hidden beneath the joists.)

Careful Attention Is Paid to Crowns

While one crew member works on the layout, another sorts and crowns the joist stock (see the top left photo on p. 54). We use only kiln-dried lumber for floor joists. Kiln-dried lumber is less likely than green lumber to shrink or to change shape over time. And

A crew member sights each joist to determine the direction of the crown (left). An arrow is then drawn on the board to indicate the top edge of the board (above).

cases, the straightest A-joists are used as rim joists and beneath tiled areas such as kitchens and baths. Floor sections that will be covered with hardwood receive B-joists, and C-joists with the biggest crowns are saved for floor areas under carpet or to be cut into headers.

because kiln-dried lumber is preshrunk, we don't get problems usually associated with green stock, such as drywall cracks, cracked tile, and doors and windows that bind.

Every piece of sawn dimensional lumber has a crown, or a natural curve it takes on after it is cut from a log. We look at each floor joist and mark the direction of its crown with an arrow (see the photo above right). Those with excessive crowns (more than ¼ in. in 8 ft.) are set aside to be cut into window or door headers later.

When we get a unit of joist stock that has many boards with crowns of more than ¼ in., we grade each joist with an A, B, or C designation. Without this extra effort, we could end up with large differences between adjacent joists, creating a washboard effect in the floor and making it difficult to install the tongue-and-groove sheathing. In those

The Rim Is Installed First

The rim joist or band joist is toenailed to the outer perimeter of the floor on top of the sill plates or to the top plates of exterior walls (see the top photo on the facing page). We use 16d nails every 12 in. The rim joists that run perpendicular to the layout prevent the floor joists from rotating. Rim joists that run parallel to the layout close off the floor area along its outside edge. We also install band joists at the interior transition points where joists change direction. Here, they serve as a break point for the edges of the sheathing as well.

We select straight stock for the rim joists so that the crowns don't leave a space between the rim and the plate. If such a space is left, the rim will eventually settle under the weight of the house and cause

problems later. When straight stock is scarce, we make a sawcut near the middle of the rim joist about two-thirds of the way across the board (see the photo at right). The cut is made in the direction of the crown and lets us fasten the joist down all the way to the plate.

We use the rim joists as in-floor headers over window and door openings in framed walls wherever possible. In-floor headers let us skip the traditional headers and jack studs for openings in exterior walls that run parallel to the joist direction. As long as the rim doesn't break over the opening, a single rim joist can carry the wall weight above short openings. For wider spans such as over a sliding door, we double up the rim over the opening.

This method uses a little less lumber framing, and more important, it increases the thermal efficiency of the wall. On this house we eliminated 24 jack studs (or 3 ft. of solid wood in the walls) and 36 ft. of header stock. All this space can now be insulated.

Rim joist goes on first. Before any common joists are installed, a rim joist or band joist is nailed to the outer edge of the mudsills. While one crew member assembles the rim, another transfers the layout up from the sills to the inside face of the rim joist.

Taking the crown out of a rim joist. If a rim joist has a severe crown, a relief cut is made that allows the joist to be drawn all the way down to the sill or plate.

Using measurements written on the sills during layout, kits containing all the framing members for floor openings such as stairs or chimneys are cut and labeled ahead of time.

Common Joists Are Rolled into Place

We used to take care to cut the rim-joist stock to break exactly on the center of a floor joist. But because the structural wall sheathing extends down to cover and secure the joint, there isn't any real benefit in doing so. We do check the end of every rim joist to make sure that it's square and trim it if it's not. Square ends are especially critical at the corners to maintain the exact dimensions of the floor deck. Once all the rim joists are in place, we use a framing square or a triangular rafter square to square up all the layout lines from the sills or basement wall plates onto the inside of the rims.

The crew member who crowns the floor joists also checks the end that will butt against the rim joist for square. At the same time, framing members for floor openings are cut from the measurements written on the sill plates and then grouped into kits (see the photo at left). For example, the kit for this house's chimney consisted of short rim-joist pieces, headers, and cripple joists.

When the kit is finished and each piece is clearly marked, it is neatly stacked outside the foundation close to where it will be installed. In areas where joists change direction, the joists have to be cut to length to fit between two rim joists. After being cut, these joists are also stacked near where they will be installed.

We usually assign one crew member to assemble and install the kits for rough floor openings, and the rest of the crew installs the common joists. We first lay all the joists flat on the sill plates and across the carrying beams with all the crowns facing in the same direction (see the photos on pp. 50–51). Now we can walk along the outside of the foundation or on top of the plate rolling the joists into place and nailing them to the rim (see the photo below).

If a joist is shorter in height than the rim, we lift and nail it flush with the top of the rim. We go back later and shim under all the short joists. After a joist is nailed through the rim with four or five 16d nails, we drive three toenails through the joist and into the mudsill or top plate. At this point, however,

Rolling the joists into place. After the joists are laid in flat, a crew member rolls them onto their layout marks and nails them to the rim.

we don't nail the joists at the beams or bearing walls.

After all the joists are nailed in place, we recheck the strings that we set up earlier to straighten all the interior carrying beams and walls as well as any exterior framed walls. When we're satisfied that everything is straight, we walk the beams and nail the overlapping joists to each other again, flushing the tops and shimming under short joists. The overlapping joists are fastened to each other with four or five nails driven at an angle so that the nail points don't stick out the other side. The joists are now set on the outside lines we drew earlier and toe-nailed to the beams or wall plates with four nails.

According to the 1995 Council of American Building Officials (CABO) code, each joist must bear a minimum of 1½ in. where it sits on a carrying beam, and there must be a positive connection at the joist laps. There are three basic ways to make an approved connection between joists that overlap. The most common way to connect opposing joists is by overlapping them a minimum of 3 in. Another method is using either a wooden block or steel connector plate as a splice across the joist joint. The third method is letting the subfloor sheathing span across the intersection of the joists by a minimum of 3 in.

We never use solid blocking between joists over the beams or bearing walls to transfer loads. Instead, we frame all our walls so that the studs line up directly over the joists. Wherever we have concentrated loads falling on a joist from a wall above, such as jacks carrying a load-bearing header, we install squash blocks, a technique we borrowed from our engineered-I-joist experience. Squash blocks are 2x blocks cut slightly longer than the height of the joist. They are installed on end beside the joist to help transfer loads to the sill plate or carrying beam (see the photo above). Usually, we install squash blocks after the floor is sheathed, unless we can pinpoint bearing

Squash blocks carry loads from above. Two-by blocks called squash blocks cut slightly longer than the height of the joist help to transfer loads directly to the sill plate or carrying beam. Here, the squash blocks are installed under header-bearing jacks for a sliding door above.

points before. Since we began using squash blocks in conventional floor decks, we've virtually eliminated drywall cracks around door and window openings.

Don't Skimp on the Glue for the Sheathing

When all the joists are fastened in place, we double-check all the floor-deck dimensions and take diagonal measurements to make sure the deck is square before we start installing the subfloor sheathing. If the rim joists were installed with square ends at the corners, our measurements are usually close. If the diagonal measurement is off more than ¼ in., we tweak the rim in or out to make the adjustment.

Next, we run strings along all the rim joists running perpendicular to joist runs. We tap the top of the rim in or out as needed and shim if necessary to get the rim joist perfectly straight (see the photo on p. 58). Squaring the joist ends helps to keep these adjustments to a minimum. Rims running parallel to the joists will be straightened later, after the sheathing is installed.

To begin sheathing the deck, we measure 4 ft. in at both ends from our starting edge,

Tweaking the rim joist. Before the sheathing goes on, a string is run along the top edge of all the rims that run perpendicular to the joists. The rim is tapped in or out and checked with a square until it is perfectly straight.

Start spreading the glues. A generous bead of construction adhesive is spread on each joist and on the plywood edge.

usually the front of the house. We snap a line and start pumping adhesive onto the joists. From there we snap lines every 47½ in. for a glue guide for each row of sheathing. (We use a 47½-in. measurement because the tongue and the groove cost us ½ in. for each row of sheathing.) The snapped line tells us where to stop the glue for each row to keep glue off our tapes and to keep the joists beyond the sheathing safe to step on.

The first set of sheets is set with the tongues on the rim joist so that we don't ruin them when we bang the sheets into place on successive rows. The first course of sheathing is nailed off completely with 8d ring-shank nails so that it doesn't drift when we drive the next set of sheets in place. We don't glue or nail the edges of the sheets

along the rim joist running parallel to the joist direction so that it can be straightened out later.

Spreading glue on the joists is an often-overlooked operation. However, we take our gluing seriously. We probably go through many more tubes than most crews, but we believe it's worth the extra labor and material.

Each joist gets a generous bead of glue, and the section of joist where two panels meet gets a bead along both edges of the joist (see the photo above right). We also run a bead of glue down the groove before installing the next row of sheets. The glued tongue-and-groove seams are much stiffer and squeak-free than those left dry. Plus, when glued properly, the sheathing functions as a vapor barrier, provided that all utility penetrations are carefully sealed.

Framing crews usually just flop the sheets of sheathing down haphazardly onto the joists and slide them over into position. In the process, the glue is smeared and rendered useless, and the joists become a sticky, slippery mess. Instead, we try to lay each sheet down as close to where it is supposed to go and as carefully and gently as possible, which keeps the glue bead where it belongs and keeps the work area neat and safe.

A sledgehammer snugs the sheathing into place. A 2x block protects the grooves in the edges of the sheathing as it is tapped into place with a sledgehammer.

As each sheet is laid down, it is tapped against the adjacent sheets with a 2x block and a sledgehammer (see the photo above). The OSB floor sheathing we use lies flat, and the tongues slide easily into the grooves. When plywood is specified, it's usually necessary to have an extra crew member stand on the seam to flatten the sheet. We adjust the joist that falls under the end of that sheet so that half or about ¾ in. of the joist is left exposed. The outermost corner of the sheathing is then nailed to secure the joist in position. After each course of sheathing is tacked in place in this manner and before the next course is started, we hook a tape onto any of the secured joists and measure, adjust, and nail the rest of the joists at their proper 16-in. o. c. position with a single nail at the edge of the sheathing (see the photo at right).

We stagger the butt joints between sheets 4 ft. with each successive course. When the layout approaches an area where the joists overlap, we install 2x blocking to support the end of the sheet as needed (see the left photo on p. 60). After we've tacked the whole field of sheets in place, we snap lines

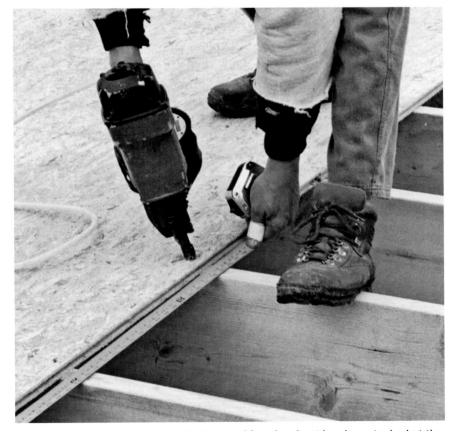

A single nail keeps the joist on the layout. After the sheet has been tacked at the corners, a tape is hooked on the joist tacked to the sheathing, and the other joists are moved until they fall into position. A single nail is then driven to hold the joist on the layout.

to indicate joist locations, taking care to shift our lines where the joists overlap or change direction (see the photo at right). One crew member then finishes all the nailing so that he can keep track of what's been nailed.

Tying Up Loose Ends

Whenever our sheathing runs by an opening such as the stair chase or the opening for the chimney, we either let a small section of sheathing overhang or leave a small uncovered area to begin the next sheet at the edge of the opening. With the bulk of the floor sheathed, we now turn to these details, trimming and filling in as needed.

Because the sheets of sheathing are 47½ in. wide, we end up with a 5-in. void at the end of our 44-ft. house. Rather than sacrificing several sheets of sheathing for their tongues, we cut up scrap pieces of sheathing and use them as fillers. The unsupported joint is not

a concern because it will be covered by the 2x6 walls above.

It's rare to have a floor this wide. Most of the houses we do are less than 30 ft. wide, so the sheathing shortfall is usually 3 in. or less. If we don't have enough scrap sheathing to use as a filler strip, we use 1x3 strapping or rip a 1x6 ledger instead, which is cheap and easy to use.

The last step is straightening the rim joists that were left unnailed during the sheathing operation (see the top photo on the facing page). Measuring in 1½ in. from the corners at the ends of the rim, we snap a reference line on top of the sheathing. We

Straightening the final edge. When all the sheathing has been installed, a line is snapped 1½ in. from the ends. The rim joist is then moved in or out until it lines up with the end of the tape.

now move the rim joist in or out every 4 ft. or so until the distance from our line to the outside edge of the rim measures 1½ in., and we drive a nail at that point. After the edge is tacked straight, we nail it off and trim off any excess sheathing.

The second-story floor deck is built pretty much the same way. However, one step that we take just before lifting the bearing walls that will support the next floor is laying out for the joists on top of the top plate, which is quicker than doing the layout from staging. Once the walls are up, we start the process of installing rims and joists all over again.

Rick Arnold and Mike Guertin are builders, remodelers, and contributing editors to Fine Homebuilding. *Rick is the author of* Working with Concrete *(2003)*

Just Say No to Bridging

Here in the Northeast, where construction quality is often judged by how much wood you can pack into a house frame, omitting bridging is a controversial choice. Unless we exceed the 6:1 (depth-to-thickness) ratio in our joist material (2x12) where the CABO code requires blocking or bridging between joists, we almost never install it.

To the best of our knowledge, bridging has never been proved to strengthen to a floor, but it is almost certain to add squeaks. In the past we tried gluing in solid blocks, and for several years we installed steel bridging as an alternative to blocking. We'd install the steel bridging tighter than a guitar string only to return a year later and find it had loosened and was causing squeaks. Even though we use kiln-dried material, the seasonal changes in humidity cause the joists to shrink and swell enough to render any type of bridging worthless.

We can just about guarantee a squeak-free floor in our homes unless our clients or an architect insists on blocking or bridging. In those cases, we are inevitably called back a year later to fix floor squeaks. The remedy for the squeaks usually involves removing any solid blocks or bridging that didn't have to be removed when the plumbers and HVAC installers did their work.

Instead, ¾-in. tongue-and-groove structural sheathing glued and nailed to the joists is effective at transferring loads to adjacent joists, which is what blocking and bridging are supposed to do. As extra insurance, we install a continuous 1x3 strap nailed to the underside of the joists down the center of the span in the basement to keep the joists from twisting. If the ceiling is to be finished, such as above a living space, we install 1x3 strapping 16 in. o. c. across the whole ceiling.

Parallel-Chord Floor Trusses

■ BY E. KURT ALBAUGH

Once associated more with commercial construction, structural trusses are becoming increasingly popular among homebuilders. Though most builders are familiar with roof trusses, fewer builders realize that floor trusses can be used quite effectively in residential construction, too. They offer a number of structural and economic advantages, and they can easily be incorporated into the design of a home without significantly changing the way a builder builds.

Structural Advantages of Trusses

Traditionally, the size of rooms in a home has been based largely on the span limitation of standard wood joists. Floor trusses with the same depth as joists can be used over longer spans, and this means that rooms can be larger, with less space obstructed by columns or unnecessary partitions. Trusses have a much greater variety of depths than wood joists do, and therefore a much wider range of spans and strength.

Trusses rarely warp. With a joist floor, natural warpage in the members can lead to an uneven floor deck. This problem can be reduced somewhat by culling out the warped joists before installation, but that increases wood waste.

Another advantage of floor trusses is that they permit ducting, plumbing, and electrical service to be run easily between the open webs. With a joist floor system, holes must often be cut through each joist in order to run electrical and plumbing lines.

Since floor trusses are sized by the fabricator, they're delivered to the job site in lengths that meet the specific requirements of the project. With joists, the material must often be cut on site to fit, which wastes wood and increases the handling of material. Installation of a truss is relatively easy, because the truss edge is 3½ in. wide. This makes it more stable while it rests on the wall plates, and easier to nail to.

A floor-truss system is engineered, while a joist system usually isn't. This means that greater floor loads can usually be carried, and deflections are better controlled. Engineering also makes for a more efficient use of material (strength vs. weight), resulting in a lower per-square-foot cost.

Strong and efficient floor trusses may someday replace wood joists as the builder's favorite floor frame.

Parallel-Chord 4x2 Floor Trusses

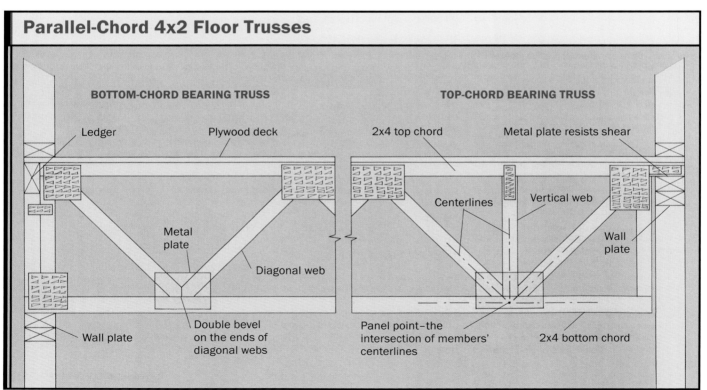

BOTTOM-CHORD BEARING TRUSS

Ledger

Plywood deck

Metal plate

Diagonal web

Wall plate

Double bevel on the ends of diagonal webs

TOP-CHORD BEARING TRUSS

2x4 top chord

Metal plate resists shear

Centerlines

Vertical web

Wall plate

Panel point–the intersection of members' centerlines

2x4 bottom chord

Cost Advantages of Trusses

The builders I've worked with who use floor trusses believe that a floor-truss system is cost-effective. But exactly how much so is difficult to determine since labor and material costs vary greatly throughout the United States. As a general rule for the Houston area, material costs are about 90¢ per sq. ft. of floor (with trusses 24 in. o.c.). If the job is a long way from the manufacturer, shipping can increase the costs significantly. A joist floor system, on the other hand, costs about 85¢ per sq. ft. on floor. This means that material costs for a truss floor are about 6% higher than for a joist floor system. But when the time saved for installing a truss floor (as much as 40%) is taken into account, the truss floor turns out to be about 10% less expensive overall.

What are the time savings? Quicker framing means a faster construction schedule, with attendant savings on construction financing. And because plumbers can route the pipes through the open webs of the trusses, no time is wasted by having to bore holes through joists. The electrician and HVAC (heating, ventilation, and air conditioning) installers save time as well. Exactly how much time each tradesperson saves is hard to determine, but it can add up over the course of a job.

On the production side, most wood-truss fabricators find that there is little difference in production costs between 12-in.-, 14-in.-, and 16-in.-deep trusses, so these tend to be comparable in cost to the builder. But when trusses get deeper than 16 in. material costs increase significantly because web material other than #3 shorts must by bought (now you know where mill ends go).

After pricing a lot of wood-chord trusses here in the Houston area, I quickly found out that the size of a builder's truss order is the greatest single factor affecting the cost of trusses. If there are several truss fabricators in your area, each one may have a different business approach. One supplier will probably favor small-quantity, custom truss orders while another will specialize in mass production and large orders. Shopping around for the best price often means shopping for the fabricator whose business most fits yours.

Truss Anatomy

A floor truss has only three components—chords, webs, and connector plates. Each one is critical to the function of the truss. The wood chords, or outer members, are held rigidly apart by wood or metal webs. The strength-to-weight ratio of floor trusses is higher than that of solid-wood joists because the structural configuration of the truss converts the bending moments and shear forces (produced by loading) into compressive and tensile forces. These forces are directed through the individual truss members and transferred to walls.

CHORDS

The type of floor truss used most frequently in residential floor systems is called the parallel-chord 4x2 truss. As shown in the illustrations on p. 63, the chords are evenly spaced from each other. This configuration increases the structural efficiency of shallow trusses and provides them with a larger bearing area on wall plates. It also gives trusses additional lateral rigidity to resist damage during transport and installation.

In residential construction, a floor truss will most often bear on the underside of its bottom chord (see the illustration at left on p. 63), just as a joist bears on its bottom edge. But because of the structural versatility of a truss, it can also be designed to bear on the underside of its top cord. In this case, the bottom chord is shortened and the truss hangs between walls, instead of resting on top of them (see the illustration at right on p. 63). This can be a useful feature when the overall height of a building is restricted. But since height isn't usually a problem in residential construction, top-chord bearing trusses are seen more frequently in commercial work.

Chords can be made of spliced lumber as long as a metal connector plate is used to join the pieces. Chords are kiln-dried, and in the southern United States, they're generally made from No. 1 KD southern yellow pine. Truss fabricators commonly use either machine stress-rated lumber or visually graded lumber for truss chords, depending on the cost and availability of the lumber grade. During its early years, the wood-truss industry used only visually graded lumber, and trusses were designed conservatively to compensate for substantial variations in the strength and stiffness properties of the wood. Some time ago, engineers at Purdue University developed a technique to test and grade lumber by machine. Lumber graded by this process is call machine stress-rated (MSR) lumber, and truss fabricators are using it with increasing frequency for chord stock. Because every piece of MSR lumber is mechanically tested for stiffness and given a categorical strength rating, trusses can be designed to maximize the use of the wood's strength.

WEBS

The members that connect the chords are called webs. Diagonal webs primarily resist the shear forces in the truss, and they are usually positional at 45° to the chords. Vertical webs, which are placed perpendicular to the chords, are used at critical load-transfer points where additional strength is required. They also are used to reduce the loads going through the diagonal members.

Since the strength of the webs is not as critical as is the strength of the chords, a lower-quality wood can be used, such as #3 KD southern pine. Wood is the material used most frequently for webs, but metal webs are also used. Metal webs are stamped for 16-ga., 18-ga., or 20-ga. galvanized steel.

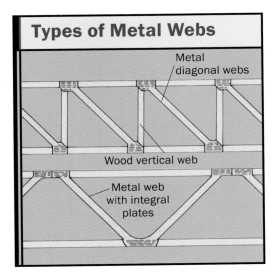

Types of Metal Webs

Metal diagonal webs

Wood vertical web

Metal web with integral plates

Several truss manufacturers have designed the metal web to incorporate a connecting plate, thus reducing the number of pieces required to assemble the truss, as shown in the illustration above. Metal-web trusses provide greater clear spans for any given truss depth than wood-web trusses. The opening between the webs is larger, too, which allows more room for HVAC ducting. And they're lighter, so they are easier to install. But a major disadvantage of metal-web trusses is that a wide range of truss depths isn't always available. Also, metal webs are more susceptible to damage during transport and installation.

In a truss with wood webs, the ends of the diagonal webs are double-beveled wherever they meet a vertical web and the chord. There is an important structural reason for this cut. The objective in the design of any truss is for the centerlines of the chord and adjoining pairs of webs to intersect at one point. This is called the panel point. When centerlines don't intersect at a panel point, additional and undesirable stresses are introduced at the joint.

There are several different types of parallel-chord floor trusses, and what makes each one different is the arrangement of its webs. Depending on their arrangement, the webs will be either in compression or tension, and this dictates how loads are transferred from the truss to the structure supporting it. Pratt, Howe, and Warren trusses were named after their respective developers. Howe and Pratt designed their trusses for railroad bridges. Two giant timber-framed trusses could span a river or a canyon, and trains would run over tracks that stretched alongside the bottom chords.

CONNECTOR PLATES

In 1952, A. Carol Sanford invented the toothed metal connector plate, which eliminated the need for nailing and gluing truss plates. Metal connector plates substantially reduced the cost of trusses by allowing them to be mass produced.

Variations of the toothed connector plate are now commonly used to assemble trusses. They are made from 16-ga., 18-ga., and 20-ga. hot-dipped galvanized steel, which is punched to form numerous metal prongs, or "teeth," that extend outward from one side of the plate. When embedded in the wood of the truss (usually by a hydraulic press), these teeth give the plate its holding power. Specifications for designing trusses using metal connector plates are available from the Truss Plate Institute®, Inc. They also distribute test and research data.

If you've had a chance to examine connector plates, you may have noticed that they are not always the same size. As they increase in size, they provide more embedded teeth, and therefore more holding power. Larger plates are used in joints with higher stresses.

Deflection

The design of a truss is usually governed more by bending limitations than by anything else. Too much bending, or deflection, can make a floor noticeably springy and result in cracks in the finished ceiling below. The American Institute of Timber Construction recommends deflection limitation for trusses of L/360 for the live-load portion of the total load and L/240 for the total load, where L is the span in inches. Live loads are calculated only if they are expected to be unusual—for example, placing a pair of pianos on the second floor. Generally, though, the total load calculation is used. Total load includes the weight of everything attached to or bearing on the top and bottom chords. It includes the dead weight of floor and ceiling materials, as well as the live loads of people, pianos, and furniture.

To see how deflection limitations are used, suppose a floor truss must be selected to span 22 ft. between two walls. The maximum allowable total load deflection is calculated by converting the span distance to inches (22 x 12 = 264) and dividing this by 240. So a truss must be selected that will deflect no more than 1.1 in. at mid-span. In other words, if the truss is subjected to all loads anticipated, the most it may deflect downwards is 1.1 in. Remember that this is total deflection, including that caused by dead weight; it doesn't mean that every footstep will cause the truss to deflect 1.1 in.

Deflection limitations provide design parameters for the engineer in selecting an appropriate truss. Knowing the maximum deflection allowable over a particular span, the engineer can determine a truss depth that will deflect less than the maximum allowable distance. This can be done by mathematical calculation or by consulting data from truss-plate manufacturers concerning their products.

A floor system consists of the deck material and supporting network of trusses, and both components function together to transfer floor loads to the walls and foundation. But when trusses are engineered for a particular application, the effect of the deck material on truss stiffness is not taken into account. The floor-system strength is based solely on the stiffness of the truss itself. Because of this, the deflection calculations are on the conservative side.

Choosing a Truss

Figuring the total loading on a floor system involves some calculation, but you don't necessarily have to hire an engineer or an architect to size trusses for your project. Engineering is provided either by the truss fabricator or by the plate manufacturer whose plates are purchased by the truss fabricator. These people work together to ensure that the combinations of plates, webs, and chords are structurally sound.

To size a truss, the fabricator will first review your plans and look for any unusual circumstances that could affect the truss design. If nothing unusual is found, the truss design and depth will be chosen from reference manuals supplied by the plate manufacturer. These manuals list the standard truss designs and include span tables for each. The span tables simplify all the engineering variables into a very usable form, and are based on design formulas that come from actual laboratory tests of trusses. Spans are listed for four commonly used truss spaces: 12 in., 16 in., 19.2 in., and 24 in. The most common spacing for residential construction is 24 in., but trusses can be placed at any spacing that will allow the floor system to carry the loads specified in the building codes. All the spans listed in the tables assume the deflection limitations of L/360 and L/240.

Since truss-plate size is a critical factor in truss design, the plate manufacturer will often supply pre-certified engineering for the trusses, stating the limitations with in which they will meet certain performance standards, such as the deflection limitations.

If a standard design can be found to meet your needs, the truss fabricator will provide you with a certified drawing of it. Proof of this certification is the engineer's stamp on each page of the drawing.

If the design of your structure is unusual, with particularly long spans, heavy loads, or unusual support conditions, it may call for a floor truss that has to be engineered

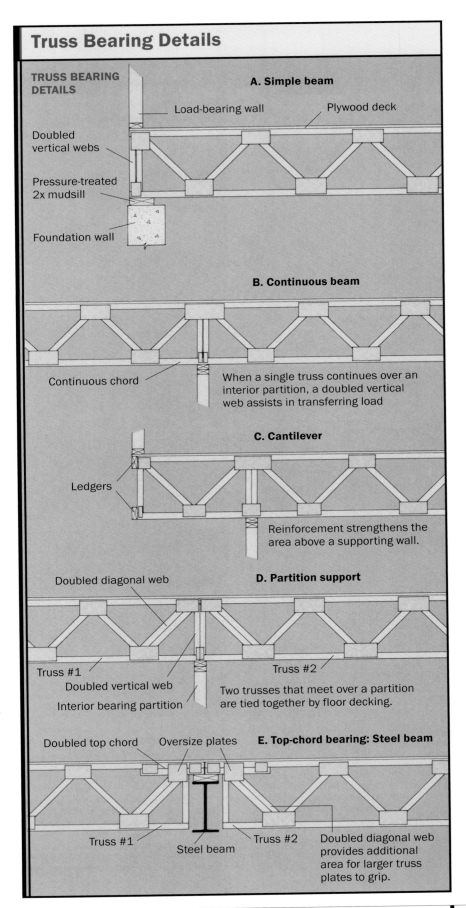

Truss Bearing Details

TRUSS BEARING DETAILS

A. Simple beam

Load-bearing wall
Plywood deck
Doubled vertical webs
Pressure-treated 2x mudsill
Foundation wall

B. Continuous beam

Continuous chord
When a single truss continues over an interior partition, a doubled vertical web assists in transferring load

C. Cantilever

Ledgers
Reinforcement strengthens the area above a supporting wall.

D. Partition support

Doubled diagonal web
Truss #1
Truss #2
Doubled vertical web
Interior bearing partition
Two trusses that meet over a partition are tied together by floor decking.

E. Top-chord bearing: Steel beam

Doubled top chord
Oversize plates
Truss #1
Steel beam
Truss #2
Doubled diagonal web provides additional area for larger truss plates to grip.

specifically for your project. In this case, you'll need to arrange for an outside engineer to do the calculations.

Typically, parallel-chord floor trusses with wood webs are available in depths ranging from 12 in. to 24 in., in 1-in. increments. The most common depths are 14 in. and 16 in. One plate manufacturer has designed a metal-web truss with the same actual depth dimensions as 2x8, 2x10, and 2x12 solid-wood joists. These smaller sizes are interchangeable with an ordinary joist floor system.

The amount of space between webs is another thing to consider when you choose a truss. When ducts will be routed under the floor, the depth of the truss may be dictated by the size of the ducts. Usually this isn't a problem, since most fabricators have a standard truss design that includes a chase opening. To create a chase opening, one web in midspan is removed to provide space for large ducts. The truss doesn't collapse on account of the missing web because shear forces are minimal at midspan.

One last note about choosing trusses. Before you leave the fabricator's office, make sure that your order is complete. If you run short of joists, you can dash off to the lumberyard. But since trusses are precisely fabricated to your specifications, you will probably have to reorder the ones that you forgot. This can be expensive and time-consuming as well.

Truss Bearing Details

A critical aspect of a floor-truss design and installation is the amount and location of bearing surfaces, since the accumulated loads of the truss are concentrated here. Bearing details vary, depending on how and where the truss is being used.

For the simple-beam condition (see illustration A on p. 67), the truss is supported at each end, and rests on its lower chord, in joist fashion. It can also rest on its upper chord, and will carry the same amount of weight as an otherwise identical bottom-chord bearing truss.

A floor truss designed as a continuous beam will be supported on each end, as well as at one or more points in between. To ensure proper load transfer at the intermediate support points (a column or partition, perhaps), a vertical web member should be located directly over the bearing area (see illustration B on p. 67). Some truss fabricators will identify the intermediate load-bearing points on a continuous-span truss by stapling a green or red warning note to the area. These warnings are particularly helpful when you install the truss, since they help position the truss and keep you from accidentally installing it upside down.

When floor trusses are to be cantilevered (see illustration C on p. 67) to support a balcony, for example, it is particularly important that provisions be made for extra support at the bearing points (see the photo above).

Floor trusses can be cantilevered over longer distanced than wood joists. These trusses will support a balcony. Pressure-treated wood was used for the end web as a precaution against rot caused by possible water infiltration. The double vertical web member at the wall provides additional support for the deck loads on the cantilever.

The truss should always be designed so that a panel point rests over a bearing point. This transfers the load from the truss directly to the supporting element. To strengthen the area even more, the bottom and top chords can be doubled near the support point of the cantilever.

Trusses can also be used in multiples. In illustration D on p. 67, two of them meet over an interior partition, while in illustration E, a steel beam provides the intermediate support.

Strengthening Trusses

When floor systems are designed, the usual approach is to specify a single truss depth that will work from the entire system, regardless of the various span distances. This simplifies material orders and eliminates the possibility of mix-ups at the job site. Situations do arise, however, when it isn't practical or cost-effective to increase the depth of all the trusses in order to beef up just a few, and in these cases the truss fabricator can increase the stiffness of individual trusses.

Chords can be strengthened across the entire length of the truss by reinforcing the top and bottom chords with a second layer of wood, fastened into place with metal plates, nails, and glue. Side-by-side floor trusses are often used to carry greater floor loads (see the photo on p. 71), in a technique akin to sistering wood joists. Other options include using larger truss plates, stronger wood for the chords, or doubled webs in critical shear areas of the truss.

Sometimes floor trusses have a slight lengthwise curve that's built into them by the manufacturer. This curve is called *camber*, and it helps to eliminate the visual effects of deflection and to control cracking.

Before the decking is nailed down, trusses should be measured at midspan to make sure they haven't swayed out of alignment (note the tape measure in the photo). A pair of 2x4s can then be nailed to the trusses at the chase opening to ensure that the top and bottom chords stay at the proper spacing. These 2x4s are not strongbacks, however; strongbacks are usually 2x10s or 2x12s.

area, visit their production shops or look at samples of their work at job sites before you buy.

When you examine webs and cords, look at their alignment. Make sure that the centerlines of all the members intersect at a panel point, and that this point is adequately covered by a truss plate. Take a close look at the wood joints, too. They should be closely fitted. Truss-plate teeth should be evenly embedded into the wood for proper load transfer.

Installing Floor Trusses

A certain amount of care must be taken when installing floor trusses, but otherwise the installation isn't much different from the installation of wood joists. When trusses are delivered to the job site, be sure to check them against the design drawings. Any structural peculiarities, like bearing blocks or doubled chords, should be verified. A bearing block is the extra vertical web that's put in a truss over any support point. Watch for the identification tags on the truss to help you find the bearing blocks.

Metal-web trusses should be inspected carefully to ensure that no webs have been bent. As a general rule, most metal-web trusses are designed to put the webs in tension, so a bent web is not always a problem. But it's best not to take chances. Wood webs should be checked for looseness or damage, as should the plates.

As a rule, the truss fabricator will deliver the trusses to the job site. Make sure you have enough help on site to unload and place the trusses. Be careful when handling them because the edges of a sharp truss plate or metal web can cut. Wear gloves.

Some builders have told me that the reason they don't like to use trusses is because they have to hire a crane to lift large ones into position. I firmly believe that even large trusses can be moved by hand up to first-floor wall plates, though the task is a little

But camber does not add strength—it's simply a matter of appearance.

A common way to strengthen a floor system is to install a strongback, usually a 2x10 or 2x12, between the web openings to help distribute loading to adjacent trusses. Sometimes two 2x4s are slipped on edge through the web openings of a series of trusses at midspan, and then nailed to a vertical web member, as shown in the photo above. This doesn't add much strength, but it helps to maintain truss alignment.

Choosing a Truss Fabricator

The strength of trusses is affected by the quality of their construction, so purchase your trusses from a reputable fabricator. If you aren't familiar with fabricators in your

After the trusses are toenailed to the top plate, a ledger is nailed in place along their top corners. This further stabilizes the floor and provides an additional horizontal nailing surface for siding. To support additional loads, particularly at the edges of floor openings, trusses can by doubled.

Sources

The American Institute of Timber Construction
333 W. Hampden Ave.
Suite 712
Englewood, CO 80110
(303) 792-9559
www.aite-glulam.corp

Truss Plate Institute, Inc.
583 D'Onofrio Dr.
Ste. 200
Madison, WI 53719
(608) 833-5900
www.tpinst.org

more difficult when you get to second-floor plates. If you decide to use a crane for the job, you might as well use it to stack the plywood up there, too. Just be sure to nail the trusses securely into place first, and be sure you don't overload them. Bottom-chord bearing trusses can be further stabilized by temporarily nailing a stringer board to the ends of the trusses.

As the trusses are being set into place, make sure they're right side up. They're sometimes installed upside down by accident, and when this happens, webs and chords that were designed for compression will be in tension. Truss failure is the likely result of this mistake.

Once the trusses have been toenailed to the wall plate (if need be you can nail through one of the holes in the connector plate) a ledger board (see the photo above) is nailed to their top edge to stabilize them

and provide a continuous horizontal nailing surface for siding. The ledger fits into a notch created for this purpose by the truss fabricator.

If the top or bottom of the truss system is to be exposed when the structure is complete, it should be permanently tied together somewhere at midspan. If the top chords are exposed to an unfloored attic, for example, the trusses should be braced with 2x material at least every 3 ft. along their length. If the bottom chords are exposed to an unfinished basement, bracing should not exceed 10-ft. intervals.

* Cost estimates are from 1986.

E. Kurt Albaugh, P.E., is a consulting engineer based in Houston, Texas.

The Well-Framed Floor

■ BY JIM ANDERSON

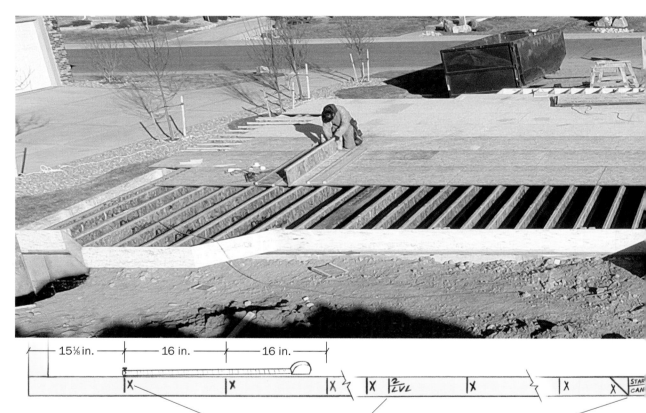

|← 15⅛ in. →|← 16 in. →|← 16 in. →|

X   X   X   X ²/LVL   X   X   X   STAR CAN

Adjust the Layout before It's Too Late

First, lay out the mudsill for the regular 16-in. o. c. joists. Then locate additional elements, such as cantilevers, stairs, plumbing drains, and large ducts. You may need to adjust the joist spacing based on these additional elements. It's easier to make changes now than later.

Begin the layout on a long, straight section of the foundation. Place the first mark 15⅛ in. from the end for a 1¾-in. I-joist (or 15¼ in. for a solid-wood joist). From there, mark every 16 in. to the other end.

Stair openings require heavier framing (often doubled-up joists). Here, two LVLs are indicated.

Cantilevers, which require joists to extend beyond the mudsill, are labeled to indicate their angle and starting point.

Walking across a newly framed floor for the first time is a milestone in any framing project. Finally, there's something to stand on that doesn't squish beneath your boots. It's flat and strong, and because there's a floor to stand on, the rest of the project will move ahead much more quickly. But whether you're using common lumber or I-joists (see the sidebar on p. 78), it takes a well-coordinated effort to get any floor to the point where you can walk on it.

Before you start driving nails, it's important to collect as much information as possible about the locations of the joists, posts, beams, point loads, cantilevers, plumbing vents, drains, and HVAC ducts on the floor-framing plan. Whether those details come from the architect, you, or somewhere else, the floor-framing plan needs to reflect the house as it's going to be built.

Having all this information in one place allows you to overlay—in pencil—the big immovable parts of the house on top of each other. This step will catch most if not all the big mistakes that can be made early on. It's a lot easier to erase than it is to remove and replace.

Whether it's the floor of a big house or a small addition, an accurate layout and efficient techniques promote smooth installation.

If a plumbing drain, furnace flue, or duct can't be moved and it's too close to a joist, move the joist. Moving it an inch or two is better than cutting the joist and framing around the pipe.

If the last joist bay is less than 12 in., make it a full 16 in. to allow plumbers, HVAC, and electricians more room.

Bearing (or squash) blocks are installed at all point loads. But to avoid confusion with other layout marks, they aren't located and installed until after the rim joist is in place.

Transfer the Details from the Plans to the Mudsills

First, I check the joist spacing on the floor-framing plan, usually 16 in. or 19.2 in. o. c. and transfer that to the mudsills. Measuring from the end of the house (usually beginning with the longest uninterrupted run), I mark the edge of the first joist 15⅛ in. from the end for 1¾-in. I-joists (16 in. minus half the joist thickness). This places the center of the first joist at 16 in.

Then I mark 16 in. o. c. (or whatever the proper spacing is) from the first mark to the other end of the house. I do this on the front and back walls, then I check the layout marks on both ends to make sure that they are the same. If they are within ¼ in., I leave it; if not, I double-check the layout and make adjustments. I also mark the location of stairs, load-bearing members, and cantilevers on the mudsill.

Leave Room for Pipes and Ductwork

If the layout mark for the last joist is within a foot of the endwall, I move it to allow room for plumbing, electrical, or HVAC in what is often an important joist bay. I usually just measure and mark 16 in. from the edge of the mudsill back toward the center of the house.

I also make sure that none of the plumbing fixtures or flue chases lands on a joist. This is another opportunity to double-check myself. It's a lot easier to move the joist now than it is to move it later or repair damage from a determined plumber with a chainsaw. I usually allow a minimum of 12 in. between joists for furnace flues, which provides 2 in. of clearance on each side for an 8-in. furnace flue. Even though 1 in. on each side meets the building code here in Denver, I figure that where heat and wood are concerned, more room is better.

Again, I create this space either by moving the joist off the 16-in. o. c. layout or,

Don't Be Afraid to Hire a Crane

Many people associate cranes only with big commercial jobs, such as skyscrapers or shopping malls. But today cranes are commonly available for residential work, and anybody can hire one.

With a crane and one helper, I can set all the steel for a house and distribute stacks of presorted materials to where they're needed. This process usually takes about 1½ hours ($180 here in Denver). This easily is cheaper than paying labor to move all that material, and we get to the framing faster.

when that isn't practical, by cutting the joist just short of the flue and supporting it with a header tied into the joists on each side of the one that's cut.

Plumbing drains and supply lines are zero-clearance items, so I can have wood right next to them. I locate the fixtures on the plan, and if a joist is on or near the centerline of the drain, I move the joist 1 in. or 2 in. in one direction or the other. If I have two fixtures close together and moving a joist away from one drain places it beneath another, I open the spacing a little more (and double the joist) so that both drains lie within a slightly oversize bay.

Prepare Material According to Where It's Needed

Wood I-joists come from the yard in a large bundle; the rim material and any LVLs usually are strapped to the top. With a helper, I move the LVLs to sawhorses for cutting to length and to install joist hangers.

We move the rim joists to the top of the sheathing or to the ground, and place stickers beneath so that we can lift them easily later. Then we square one end of all the wood I-joists with a simple jig (see the photo above); as we take them off the pile and sort them by length and location. When I finish with the I-joists, I build any LVL headers and add joist hangers if they're needed.

After the prep work is done, I usually call in a crane to set all the steel beams that will carry the first floor and to spread all the presorted stacks of joists and LVLs to their appropriate locations. I also move the sheathing to within 3 ft. or 4 ft. of the foundation so that I don't have to carry it any farther than necessary.

After placing the steel, I make sure that the layout on the beams matches what is on the walls. I check the layout by pulling a string from front to back to verify that the layout marks on the front and back walls

Square one end of each joist while sorting and stacking. Because I-joists are cut to approximate length at the lumberyard, it is easier just to square one end as you are sorting them.

intersect the marks on the beams. I also make sure that the beams are straight and flat, and make any necessary adjustments.

Spread Joists to the Layout Marks and Roll Them Upright

With one person on each side of the foundation, we quickly position the joists on their layout marks, with the square-cut end aligned on the rim-joist line snapped along the mudsill (see the top photo on p. 76). Then we tack each joist in place with an 8d nail to keep it in place. It's easier to set the joists to the line first and then install the rim joist later. After tacking down all the joists, we prepare to cut the other end of the joists in place. We snap a chalkline that

Position the square ends of each joist to the chalkline (the rim-joist line) and tack them into place along their 16-in. o.c. layout lines. Later, the 8d nail will act as a hinge when the joists are stood upright.

After aligning the joists, snap a chalkline, and cut them to length in place. Beware of anchor bolts lurking below when making this cut.

is 1⅜ in. from the outside of the mudsill, which becomes the cutline.

Cutting the joists to their finished length is as simple as running the saw along the chalkline using the I-joist cutoff guide (see the photo at left). The scrap of wood lands in front, where it's available for use as a piece of blocking.

We position one person in the front and one in the back, and starting from one end, we stand all the joists and nail them in place (see the top photo on the facing page). The 8d nail that had held the joist in place now acts as a hinge for it. We usually can stand all of the joists for 40 lin. ft. of floor in about 10 minutes.

On each end of the I-joist and at the center beam, we put one 10d nail on each side of the joist through the flange into the mudsill. We keep the nails as far from the

You can do this alone, but it sure goes quicker with two. With one person at each end, stand the joists upright and put them on their layout marks. Drive one 10d nail through the flange on each side of the joist into the mudsill (or pony wall).

end of the joist as possible to avoid splitting the I-joist's flange. After standing the joists, we add the rim boards, cutting and nailing as we work our way around the house (see the photo at right). We put one 10d nail through the rim into the top and bottom flange of each I-joist.

Once the rim joist goes up, the last thing to do before sheathing is to add bearing blocks, also known as squash blocks (see the bottom right photo on p. 57). One person details the rim joist for bearing blocks, and another follows behind and nails them in place.

Bearing blocks are required anywhere that concentrated loads land on the joists, such as doorways or where a post supports a beam. We also put them at all inside corners because 90% of the time, this spot is a bearing point.

The rim joist goes on after the joists are in place. The rim joists are cut and nailed to the mudsill every 8 in. with a 10d nail.

Why I Prefer I-joists over Solid Wood

I remember the first time I saw I-joists, those long, floppy things. They seemed so flimsy and light that I thought they would have trouble holding up the sheathing, not to mention the walls that would go on top of them.

They have more than proven me wrong, however. The main advantages are that I-joists are dimensionally stable and very straight. The web (the wide middle section) of an I-joist is cut from oriented strand board (OSB), thin strands of wood oriented in the same direction and glued together. Because glue surrounds all those strands of wood, you can expect less shrinking and swelling and very consistent joist sizes (usually within 1/16 in.).

You also can cut much larger holes into I-joists than into solid lumber; holes up to 6 in. are allowed in the center of the span of a 9½-in. I-joist. Elsewhere along the web, 1½-in. holes are provided in perforated knockouts. Holes in solid lumber can be no more than one-third the total width.

I-joists must be handled carefully; upright is best, or supported in a couple of places if carried flat. They're light, come in lengths up to 60 ft., and can span long distances as part of an engineered floor system. Best of all, they cost about the same as lumber; in the longer lengths, they actually cost less.

Stack Sheathing on the Floor as Soon as Possible

We snap the line for the first course of sheathing 48½ in. from the outside edge of the rim joist. It's held back a little from the rim to account for any inconsistency in the rim joist.

Before we begin nailing the sheathing, we look for joists that may have been moved from the 16-in. o. c. layout. If our plywood joints are able to avoid them, sheathing will go much faster. After deciding on a starting point, we spread construction adhesive on top of the joists. Then we lay the first row and two sheets of the second row (see the top left photo on the facing page). This approach creates a little staging area where we can stack the rest of the sheathing.

We sheathe over to the steel beams in the center and add any bearing blocks and joist blocking when we get there (see the top right photo on the facing page). Waiting until the floor is partially sheathed before installing blocks is a lot easier and safer than trying to balance on unbraced joists.

We cut all the blocks and spread them across the edge of the sheathing (next to the beam), starting at one end and grabbing them off the sheathing as we go. Layout marks for each joist on the plywood's edge keep the joists straight and plumb, and the spacing for blocking consistent. When we have a finished basement, we also add wall ties as we work our way across the floor, which keeps us from having to walk across unsupported joists.

When we get to a stair rough opening, we sheathe over it and brace the plywood seams. Not only is this approach safer, it also creates more usable floor space when we start framing walls. Before we stand any walls that surround the stair opening, we open it up again. If the hole is too large to sheathe over, we add a safety rail.

Lay the first row of sheathing plus two more sheets; then move the rest of the stack onto the floor. It takes about 10 minutes to move 40 sheets; it's much quicker than having to climb up and down to get every sheet.

Sheathe your way over to where blocking is needed. Do not walk across unstable joists or work from a ladder below the floor. Sheathe over to the beam, then add the joist blocking.

Lay as Many Full Sheets as Possible

As we sheathe, we lay as many full sheets as possible (making the fewest number of cuts). I've found that running the sheets long at the ends and cutting to a chalkline snapped along the rim (see the photo at right) turns out a better product than measuring and cutting the pieces to fit individually.

I pull the chalkline in an extra ⅛ in. from the outside of the rim; this eliminates ever having to cut the rim line again. One person starts at a corner of the house and snaps all the rim lines; the other follows behind with the saw. The rim joist is first straightened and then nailed to the sheathing every 6 in.

Jim Anderson is a framing contractor in Littleton, Colorado.

Cut the sheathing in place. Run sheets long at the ends, snap a chalkline, and cut off the excess. This process is faster and turns out a better floor than cutting each piece to fit.

Building Coffered Ceilings

■ BY MARK FEIRER

Editor's note: The following three projects hardly look the same, but they share one detail: a coffered ceiling. A coffer is characterized by sunken panels (they're usually square or octagonal) that decorate a ceiling or a vault. Though the term is generally associated with multiple panels, a proper coffer can have a single panel. The technique is thought to derive from the visual effect created in buildings where heavy ceiling beams crossed one another, and it has been used structurally and decoratively for buildings as dissimilar as neoclassical churches and the Washington, D. C., subway system.

Jay Thomsen used crisscrossed 1x wood strips to create the effect of sunken panels over the surface of a vaulted ceiling. Don Dunkley frames coffers into custom homes, typically by creating one big recessed panel. And Greg Lawrence used coffering to conceal glulam beams.

Three against one. The pliable nature of pine 1x stock allowed each layer of the ribbing to follow the vault of the ceiling. Nevertheless, it took a lot of work to press each strip into place.

Applied Coffer

Usually an addition is built to reflect the design of the main house. A recent project of ours, however, showed that the opposite can also be true: Eventually, the Mracheks' house will be remodeled to reflect the addition.

As vice president of the Handel and Haydn Society in Boston, Mass., Bobbi Mrachek wanted a room in which to entertain large numbers of guests, usually for live performances of classical music. The design delivered by local architect John McConnell called for a room 40 ft. by 15 ft. 16 in., topped with a barrel vault. The look of the ceiling had to be bold, but not dark and depressing, and the surfaces had to reduce the echo effect of such a large space. Coffering would soak up the echoes. To do this without further complicating an already involved ceiling structure, we created a coffered effect with strips of 1x stock.

A vault of considerable size. This room addition was designed to house live performances of classical music. The lofty, coffered ceiling was created with built-up layers of 1x stock that were painstakingly screwed and nailed into place.

Providing the Structure

As builders, we had constructed barrel vaults before, but never one so big. Given the dimensions of the room, we knew we had a serious project to contend with.

We framed the main roof of the addition as a gable with 2x10 rafters. Flush-framed collar ties (see the photo below left) secured with metal gusset plates completed the basic shape of the room. Plywood gussets would form the exact curve of the vault and provide a nail base for the finish ceiling (see the photo below right).

Calculating the radius of the plywood strips was done simply by drawing a layout on the floor to exact scale using a string, a nail, and a pencil. Sheets of ¾-in. CDX plywood were then laid out on top of the curve, and the radius was redrawn on top of the sheets. Three stacks of templates and several jigsaw blades later, we were ready to begin installation.

A Working Solution

The height of the ceiling (18 ft. 6 in.) became a factor in our planning at this point, not so much for safety reasons but for convenience: To hand each of the 1,350 pieces of the ceiling up a long ladder from below would have taken too much time. So we built a temporary second floor within the room to serve as a work platform—we'd need only a short stepladder to reach the highest point of the ceiling. A space 18 in. wide, running the length of the room, was left along each side of the platform to provide access for hoses, cords, passing up stock, and even to dangle our legs through when working at the springline of the vault (the springline is the point of the ceiling where the curve first leaves the vertical plane of the wall).

The Finish Ceiling

After screwing the plywood gussets to the rafters and touching up the resulting curves with a belt sander, it was time to start nailing up the 1x6 finish ceiling. The Mracheks didn't want to see the V-groove that would characterize the seams of conventional tongue-and-groove stock, so custom stock was milled from clear select pine. Every piece was prestained on both sides and both edges—twice—before installation and was sealed as soon as it went up.

We started the first piece of 1x6 at the centerline of the ceiling. Succeeding boards were then brought down either side toward the springlines. This allowed two crews of two men to work at the same time. We used nailers and 6d finish nails to secure the boards,

The shape revealed. The project began with standard gable-roof framing. Flush cross ties (photo at left) secured with metal plates roughed out the shape of the barrel vault. Plywood gussets (photo above) provided the final shape. They were screwed to the rafters.

toenailing most connections to avoid the incredible amount of time it would have taken to fill exposed nail holes with wood putty.

The Coffer Emerges

The main ribs of the coffering were to be layers of ½-in. pine applied in descending order of width (see the illustration below). Intersecting ribs would overlap each other. Our hopes were that the layering of each member would create enough shadow lines to stand out from the background 1x6s and make the ribs seem deeper than they were (see the photo at right). The heavier ribs that line up with the columns in the wall below are 7½ in. wide and one layer thicker than the smaller, intersecting ribs, which are 5½ in. wide. The larger ribs helped to break the ceiling into sections that were easily subdivided into smaller, coffered squares.

Fortunately, ½-in. pine conformed to the radius of the ceiling, although it took three carpenters to bend and fasten each member in place (see the photo on p. 81). Each layer, except the final one, was screwed in place with 1⅝-in. drywall screws; subsequent layers hid the screw heads. The final layer of each rib was secured with 8d finish nails. In some cases, especially near joints, we needed better holding power, so we used 1⅝-in. trim screws instead of nails. All pieces were installed with butt joints; we were afraid that the beveled ends of scarf joints might slide past each other as the layers were fastened into place.

Given the repetitive but very precise nature of the coffering, it was important to come up with an accurate,

Adding up the ribs. Stepped layers of 1x stock in various widths form the ribs of the coffer. Transverse ribs are slightly wider and one layer thicker than lengthwise ribs.

easy method for laying out the location of each member. Ribs were kept parallel to one another by constantly checking measurements off the end walls and by our consistent use of spacer sticks cut to the desired distance between ribs.

The layout of the ribs running perpendicular to the main ribs (parallel with the springline) was kept in line with a 10-ft.-long (and very flexible) layout stick, marked with the desired rib locations. As long as the end of the layout stick was butted to the springline, and the length of the stick was snug along the ceiling curve, the layout stayed very consistent. The spacing for all ribs is approximately 2 ft. o. c.

All in all, the vaulted ceiling consumed approximately 640 hours. If we had a similar ceiling to do again, we could probably cut about 50 hours from the process.

All carpentry work on this job was done by carpenters Charles Desserres (lead), Brian McCune, Don Baker, Steve Harris, and Mark Roberto of I. M. Hamrin Builders, Milton, Mass.

Jay Thomsen is a remodeling contractor in Milton, Massachusetts.

Detail of Coffer Ribs

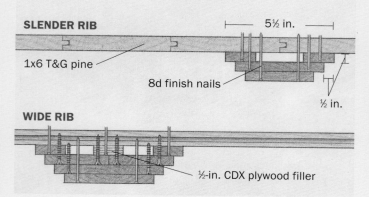

SLENDER RIB

5½ in.

1x6 T&G pine

8d finish nails

½ in.

WIDE RIB

½-in. CDX plywood filler

Single Coffer

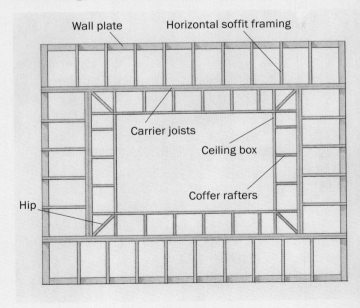

One big coffer. Soffits girdle this bedroom to support angled coffer framing. A single, recessed ceiling coffer is the result.

A common ceiling detail in custom homes is the coffered ceiling. Though the term *coffer* encompasses a range of ceiling treatments, around here we use it to refer to a ceiling with a perimeter soffit having a sloped inner face that rises to a flat ceiling (see the photo above).

The first coffers I built were usually sloped to match the roof and fastened directly to the roof framing. There was no soffit; the sloped portion of the coffer simply died into the surrounding wall, however, this method has limitations. For one thing, linking the roof to the framing of the ceiling limited the angle of the coffering to that of the roof (unless a very steep pitch was used on the main roof). Also, there was a limit to the amount of insulation that could be put into the perimeter of the coffered ceiling. Adding a soffit to the coffering solves these problems.

The soffit encircles the room and is framed so that its underside is level with the top plate. The soffit usually extends 1 ft. to 2 ft. away from the walls and offers several advantages. Framing is simplified, the pitch of the coffer can be any angle, there's plenty of room for insulation, and the flat ceiling surrounding the room can be embellished with can lights and crown molding.

The layout and the pitch of the coffer are usually found on the floor plan or the electrical plan. But before I start framing, I usually confer with the builder or the homeowner to finalize the actual size of the soffit, the pitch of the coffer, and the height of both the main ceiling and the soffit. Once these

dimensions have been confirmed, the framing can usually be completed in a few hours.

It Starts with the Soffit

One of the big advantages of the coffering technique is that the coffer framing can be done before the roof is constructed. That gives us plenty of room in which to work. The first step is to lay out the location of the doubled joists, sometimes called carrier joists, that form the outer edge of the soffit (see the illustration below). The locations are marked on the top plates of the surrounding wall. The carrier joists are oversized because they support both the coffer framing and the soffit framing—we usually use 2x10s or 2x12s, depending on the size of the room. It's important to build this part of the framing (we call it a carrier box) straight and square. Otherwise, the rest of the coffer will be a bear to build. Nail off all the carrier joists very well because green lumber, while drying, will move; three nails spread the width of the boards on 16-in. centers will suffice.

Framing Plan for Coffered Ceiling

Wall plate — Horizontal soffit framing

Carrier joists

Ceiling box

Coffer rafters

Hip

Helping fingers. Pieces of scrap stock, called fingers, should be nailed between the carrier joists and the surrounding wall framing. They prevent the joists from bowing as the soffit framing is installed. Later on, the fingers will be removed.

A topless hip. Once the soffit is in place, framing for the coffer itself is like a hip roof with the top removed. Pressure blocks are nailed between framing members on either side of the doubled carrier box; the blocks prevent the framing from twisting as it dries.

To install the carrier box, start by spanning the room (usually, but not always, the shortest dimension) with doubled carrier joists. Once these have been cut and nailed in place, string a dry line across each pair and brace them straight with a temporary 2x4 "finger." Nail the finger to the carrier, push the carrier into line, then nail off the finger to the underside of the top plate. This will hold the carrier in place until the framing is complete (see the left photo above). After lining the first two pairs of carrier joists, measure and hang (we use joist hangers) the second two pairs between them. These carrier joists should be lined and braced as well.

With the carrier box in place, you're ready to lay out the locations of soffit joists on the top plate. We use 2x4s 16 in. o. c. for these joists, running them perpendicular to all four pairs of carrier joists (see the illustration on p. 88). The soffit joists should tie into the rafters at the exterior wall plates, so lay the rafters out ahead of time.

As we toenail the soffit joists to the plate with 8d nails, we secure pressure blocks in every other bay (see the right photo above). A pressure block fits snugly between the ends of the joists to prevent them from twisting as the joists dry. Nail a 1x4 to the top of the joists that are toenailed to the plate, running it the length of the wall, and secure it with a pair of 8d nails at every joist. The 1x4 is required by code and helps to prevent twisting at the wall

end. It should be located as close as possible to the intersection of rafters and joists.

One Last Check for Clearance

With the soffit framing in place, you're ready for the angled coffer framing—but not before one last check of the specs. If the coffer is at a steeper pitch than the roof framing to follow, now's the time to make sure that the coffer framing won't interfere with the rafters. If someone changes the pitch of the roof from what's on the plans, the angle and the height of the coffer should be recalculated—a quick double-check now can avoid major problems later when the roof gets framed.

To check this, measure the run from the inside of the exterior plate (in most cases, this is where the bottom edge of the rafter will start its incline) to the inside edge of the carrier box and add this figure to the run of the coffer rafter. This gives the overall run, and by plugging this into a calculator and entering the pitch of the roof, you'll end up with the height of the roof rafter's bottom edge. When 6 in. is added to account for the thickness of the ceiling framing, you'll know if the coffer will collide with the rafters. If it will, lower the pitch of the coffer.

If the ceiling height hasn't been given on the framing plans, check a section detail (if there is one). A decent set of plans usually carries all this information. If the plans have left this information out, you'll have to calculate the height of the coffer based on the run and pitch of the coffer rafters.

The Coffer Layout

The coffer layout is no mystery; think of it simply as a hip roof with the top cut off (see the right photo on the facing page). At each corner there will be two common rafters and a hip rafter; the areas between corners will be filled with common rafters. After laying out a common-rafter pattern, we cut as many rafters as we'll need. Mark the locations on the carrier joists of all eight commons that form the coffer corners, then pick one corner and work your way around the box, installing the fill rafters. These are usually 16 in. o. c., but 2 ft. o. c. is fine if the coffer is small. We use either 2x4 or 2x6 stock. Of course, an unusually long span might call for larger stock.

Armed with the rise and run of the coffer rafters, you can figure them for length. There's no need to figure in a shortening allowance, though. When the length is known, we cut one pattern and then whack out the quantity needed. If we're building more than one coffer of the same size, the second set of rafters can also be cut now.

The Coffer Framing

After the rafters are cut (but before installing them), we build the ceiling box at the top of the coffer, which is similar to the carrier box that forms the soffit. The difference is that the ceiling box is smaller (by the run of the coffer rafters), and the framing is not doubled up. We usually frame it on the deck from 2x6 stock, then lift it into approximate position, using temporary legs to hold it up; these legs will rest on the floor. The frame should be square; carefully cut rafters will keep it straight.

Once the ceiling box is up, install a pair of common rafters at each corner to hold the box in place. Toenail the rafters top and bottom, then install the rest of the commons, adding pressure blocks to prevent the rafters from twisting later (see the bottom photo at right). When installing the rafters, make sure that they're not bowing the ceiling box; trim them if necessary.

When the commons are in, cut the hips to finish off the corners (see the top photo at right). The hips will have double cheek cuts on both ends; the cuts can be measured in place or calculated. When installing the hips, fit them in

Framing the ceiling. A ceiling box with mitered corners forms the perimeter of the ceiling. A short hip rafter with beveled plumb cuts at top and bottom connects the corners of the ceiling box to the doubled carrier box.

Blocking the rafters. With the framing complete, Dunkley works his way around the ceiling to install any last pressure blocks that might be required.

so that the drywall will follow the plane of the rafters into the center of the hip. A 6-ft. length of 1x4 makes a good straightedge to guide the hip placement. Fill in any jack rafters, if needed.

The ceiling framing is simple: Just add joists inside the ceiling box and fill in between with pressure blocks. We use 2x4s laid flat to provide backing for the ceiling drywall along the length of the ceiling box. A strongback can be run down the center of the joist span to prevent the joists from sagging.

Don Dunkley is a framing contractor in Cool, California.

Traditional Coffer

In the course of a recent remodeling project, we removed the roof from a 1,200-sq. ft. house and built a second-story addition in its place. We had to demolish the vaulted ceiling of the existing living room to make space for the new rooms above. To support those new rooms, we installed several glulam beams parallel to the exterior wall; the photo on the facing page and the illustration beow show how we coffered the ceiling to conceal the glulams.

First we wrapped each glulam on three sides with 1x Douglas fir, detailing the edges with a roundover beading bit and a router. Then we built intersecting false beams with 2x6 blocks (ripped to match the width of the glulams) and more fir. Finally, we trimmed the ceiling with crown molding. Where the molding returned off the window head casing, a striking horned cornice was created.

The resulting coffered ceiling adds a stately look to the room and nicely complements the window muntins.

Greg Lawrence is the owner of Green River Construction in Sebastopol, California.

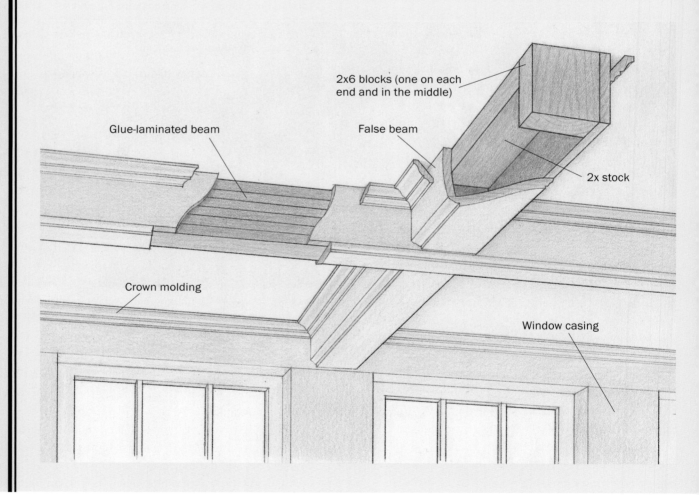

Glue-laminated beam

2x6 blocks (one on each end and in the middle)

False beam

2x stock

Crown molding

Window casing

There are several variations to our coffer-framing techniques. One way to install the ceiling box is to eliminate the temporary legs and install eight common rafters at the corners of the soffit. Then lift the ceiling box up past the commons until the bottom edge is flush with the bottom of the rafters. The pressure of the commons will hold it until everything's nailed off.

Another approach is to nail the ceiling frame to the commons one board at a time, eliminating the need for help in positioning the unit. This box is supported by the hip rafters. It can with-stand quite a load as long as the lower ceiling box is well braced with the ceiling-joist fingers.

Crown Molding

If crown molding is desired at the top of the coffer ceiling, the ceiling joists are placed on top of the ceiling box, allowing a 5½-in. recess for the molding. To blend the bottom of the coffer rafters into the inside edge of the recess, we rip the bottom edge of the ceiling box to match the rafter slope, providing a smooth transition. If the rip reduces the width of the stock too much, cut the commons with a notch to accommodate the ceiling box so that they will blend into the inside edge (the box will be oversized by 3 in. to make up for the notch).

Don Dunkley is a framing contractor in Cool, California.

Mudsills: Where the Framing Meets the Foundation

■ BY JIM ANDERSON

Framing a traditional house begins at the mudsill; it's the first piece of lumber that is attached to the foundation. If you build on a foundation that's out of square or level (and they're common), correcting the problem at the mudsill stage will make for a lot less trouble later. The first step in installing mudsills is determining if the foundation is square.

Checking for a Square Foundation

While my helper sweeps off the foundation and checks to make sure the anchor bolts are plumb, I look over the plans for the foundation's largest rectangle. It will provide an ongoing reference for establishing bump-outs (areas outside the large rectangle) and recesses (areas within the large rectangle) that are square to the house and to each other. The illustration on pp. 92–93 shows

how to square the large rectangle or to create a large 3-4-5 triangle if a rectangle can't be found.

After squaring and marking its corners, two of us snap chalklines for the large rectangle and any bump-outs or recesses, while a third person spreads pressure-treated 2x4s (or 2x6s if requested) around the foundation to serve as mudsills. Working as a team with a systematic approach is really important on these projects. We begin at the front corner and run the material along the chalkline from end to end, and then do the same in the rear. We fill in the sidewalls last.

As we work our way around the foundation, we mark the bolt locations by standing the plates on edge and outlining the bolts on the sill plate (see the top left photo on p. 94). When we have to join two mudsills, we cut the first plate within 12 in. of a bolt and add an expansion bolt for the adjacent plate. Local code requires an anchor bolt

Even if the foundation is not square or level, getting the mudsills right will get you back on track.

Square Mudsills Depend on a Square Layout

Before you can install the mudsills, you have to make sure that the foundation is square. And occasionally, foundations are a little out of square. To get the framing off to a good start, you have to snap a series of square layout lines for the mudsills. Locating and snapping lines on the foundation's largest rectangle provides a square reference for the remaining areas lying inside or outside the large rectangle. If a large rectangle can't be found, a large right triangle (see "Finding Square with Triangles" p. 94) will work.

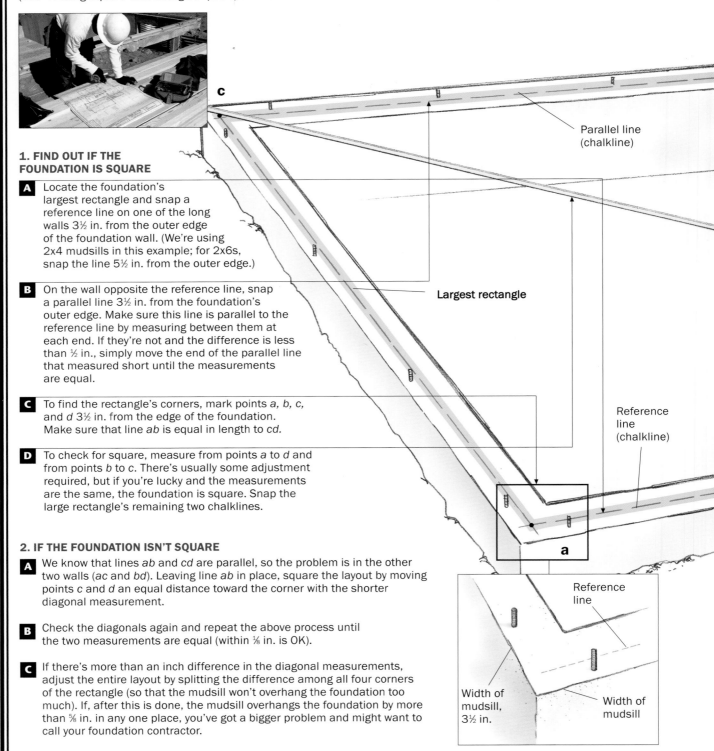

Parallel line (chalkline)

Largest rectangle

Reference line (chalkline)

a

Reference line

Width of mudsill, 3½ in.

Width of mudsill

1. FIND OUT IF THE FOUNDATION IS SQUARE

A Locate the foundation's largest rectangle and snap a reference line on one of the long walls 3½ in. from the outer edge of the foundation wall. (We're using 2x4 mudsills in this example; for 2x6s, snap the line 5½ in. from the outer edge.)

B On the wall opposite the reference line, snap a parallel line 3½ in. from the foundation's outer edge. Make sure this line is parallel to the reference line by measuring between them at each end. If they're not and the difference is less than ½ in., simply move the end of the parallel line that measured short until the measurements are equal.

C To find the rectangle's corners, mark points a, b, c, and d 3½ in. from the edge of the foundation. Make sure that line ab is equal in length to cd.

D To check for square, measure from points a to d and from points b to c. There's usually some adjustment required, but if you're lucky and the measurements are the same, the foundation is square. Snap the large rectangle's remaining two chalklines.

2. IF THE FOUNDATION ISN'T SQUARE

A We know that lines ab and cd are parallel, so the problem is in the other two walls (ac and bd). Leaving line ab in place, square the layout by moving points c and d an equal distance toward the corner with the shorter diagonal measurement.

B Check the diagonals again and repeat the above process until the two measurements are equal (within ⅛ in. is OK).

C If there's more than an inch difference in the diagonal measurements, adjust the entire layout by splitting the difference among all four corners of the rectangle (so that the mudsill won't overhang the foundation too much). If, after this is done, the mudsill overhangs the foundation by more than ⅝ in. in any one place, you've got a bigger problem and might want to call your foundation contractor.

3. LAYING OUT THE RECESSES AND BUMP-OUTS AFTER SQUARING THE LARGE RECTANGLE

Recess

Mark the lengths of each side by measuring from the main rectangle. Snap connecting chalklines.

Bump-out

A. Find the parallel line for the bump-out's outer wall by measuring from the large rectangle (as in step 1B).

B. Measuring from the closest corner of the large rectangle, mark points *g* and *h*.

C. On the outer wall, mark points *e* and *f* 3½ in. from the edge of the foundation. With each corner now marked, check for square by measuring between *e* and *h*, and between *f* and *g*. Follow the remaining steps in 1D.

D. If the bump-out doesn't have an outer parallel wall (maybe it's octagonal or circular), you can use the 3-4-5 method to find one of the two perpendicular walls, and use it as a reference line to find the other.

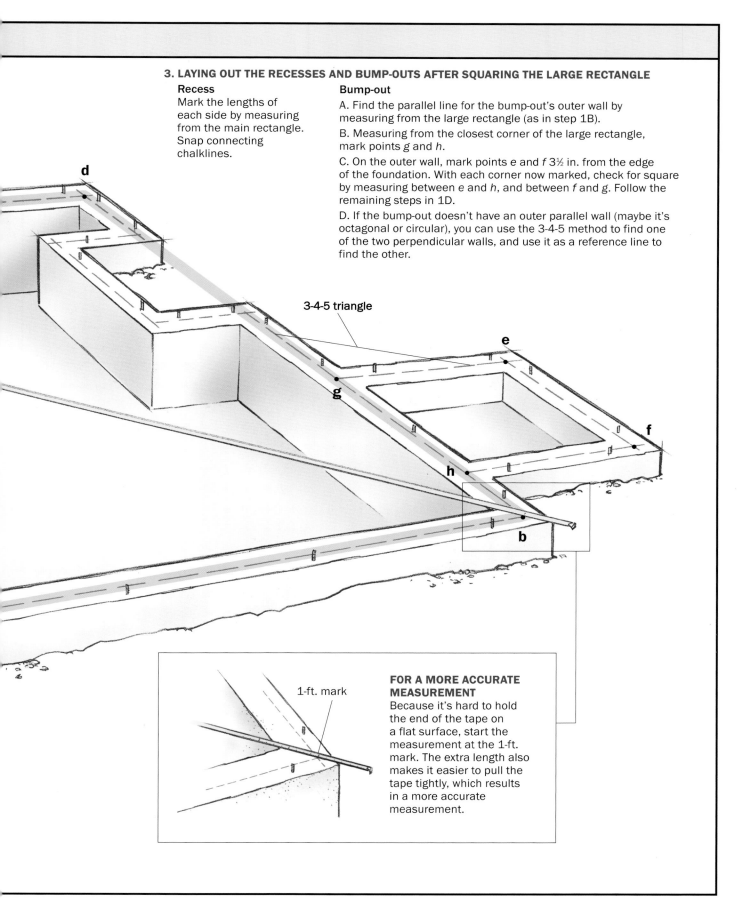

3-4-5 triangle

1-ft. mark

FOR A MORE ACCURATE MEASUREMENT

Because it's hard to hold the end of the tape on a flat surface, start the measurement at the 1-ft. mark. The extra length also makes it easier to pull the tape tightly, which results in a more accurate measurement.

Stand the sill plate on edge and trace the outline of the bolt onto the plate.

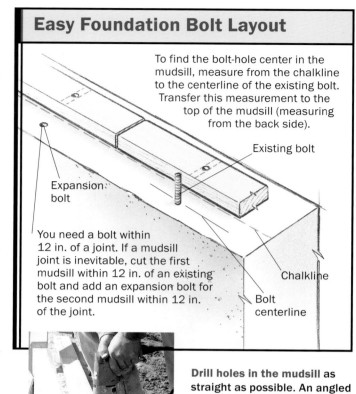

Easy Foundation Bolt Layout

To find the bolt-hole center in the mudsill, measure from the chalkline to the centerline of the existing bolt. Transfer this measurement to the top of the mudsill (measuring from the back side).

Existing bolt

Expansion bolt

Chalkline

You need a bolt within 12 in. of a joint. If a mudsill joint is inevitable, cut the first mudsill within 12 in. of an existing bolt and add an expansion bolt for the second mudsill within 12 in. of the joint.

Bolt centerline

Drill holes in the mudsill as straight as possible. An angled hole will pull the plate off the chalkline. Use a ⅝-in. bit for a ½-in. anchor bolt; place a piece of scrap lumber beneath the plate to protect the bit, or cantilever the mudsill beyond the foundation.

Finding Square with Triangles

According to the Pythagorean theorem $(a^2 + b^2 = c^2)$, any triangle with sides that measure 3-4-5 (or any multiple of these) will always have a right angle opposite the hypotenuse (side that measures 5). If a = 3, b = 4, and c = 5, and $3^2 + 4^2 = 5^2$, then 9 + 16 = 25.

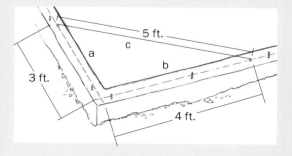

5 ft.

c

a

3 ft.

b

4 ft.

Sources

Metalwest
1229 S. Fulton Ave.
Brighton, CO 80601
(800) 336-3365
www.metalwest.com
Steel shims

Sokkia
16900 W. 118th Terr.
Olathe, KS 66051
(800) 476-5542
www.sokkia.com

Shim the Mudsills to the Stringline

The second mudsill plate raises the basement ceiling by 1½ in.

Shim with steel. Once you've established a level stringline, use steel to shim between the mudsill and foundation beneath all joist, beam, and point loads.

For a rough count, stack the shims up to the stringline in each location. Steel shims are available in 50-lb. boxes.

within 12 in. of the end of mudsills or of any joints.

Marking the bolt centers on the mudsills for drilling is next (see the inset photo on facing page). It's as simple as laying the mudsill alongside the chalkline on top of the foundation, measuring from the chalkline to the center of the bolt, and transferring the measurement to the top of the mudsills (see the illustration on facing page). At this point,

we add insulation (or sill seal if requested) between the foundation and the mudsill.

Shims Level the Mudsill; Bolts Hold It Down

After drilling the bolt holes, two of us place the mudsills over the anchor bolts and

A Builder's Level Finds the High Spots

Commonly though wrongly called a transit, a builder's level rotates only horizontally; a transit rotates both horizontally and vertically. Looking through a builder's level is like looking through a rifle scope, cross hairs and all. Properly set up, the horizontal cross hair represents a level plane, and the magnification is great enough to read a tape measure held 100 ft. away or more. A builder's level is leveled with either three or four thumbscrews and integral bubble vials. Comparing measurements taken in different spots tells you their relative elevations. But this comparison can be counterintuitive. The highest spot, being closest to the level's plane, will have the shortest measurement.

For years, I have used a builder's level to install mudsills, and although I have tried laser levels, I haven't been happy with the results. The Sokkia® E=32 level that I now own cost around $400 in 1999, and it has given me great service.

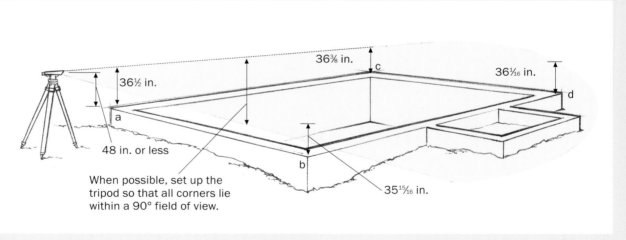

36½ in.

36⅜ in.

36¹⁄₁₆ in.

35¹⁵⁄₁₆ in.

48 in. or less

When possible, set up the tripod so that all corners lie within a 90° field of view.

another follows behind, adding nuts and washers, tightening them only enough to check for obvious high or low spots. Then we add the necessary expansion bolts at the mudsill joints and nail a second 2x4 on the mudsill. This adds an extra 1½-in. ceiling height in the basement.

Next, we use a builder's level (see the sidebar above) to measure the height of the corners and to look for any high spots. After comparing the measurements, we shim the corners to within ¹⁄₁₆ in. of the highest point on the foundation. Then we run a string

Remove high spots with an air chisel. If a high spot is really bad and it's a short length of wall, an air chisel makes quick work of a labor-intensive job.

Set-Up Tips for Best Results

1. Position the level so that you clearly see each of the foundation's corners within a relatively narrow field of view (90° or less). This helps to eliminate errors associated with swinging the level in wide arcs.

    Place the level as low to the foundation as possible. Extending the tape or measuring rod high in the air introduces error.

2. With a helper holding a tape, shoot the outside corners *a*, *b*, *c*, and *d* write their elevations on each corner. The shortest measurement is the high corner (*b*).

3. Subtract the shortest measurement from each of the other corners, and write the difference (the amount to be shimmed) at each corner.

4. Shim the corners until they measure within $\frac{1}{16}$ in. of the high corner.

5. Run stringlines from one corner to the next. For the areas between the corners, see the photo and illustration on p. 95.

from corner to corner and level the mudsills between.

When shims are necessary, the local building code requires steel shims at joist, beam, and point loads, so I mark these locations on the mudsill. After inserting the shims between the foundation and mudsill, we tighten the nuts on the anchor bolts and check the height one last time, shooting for plus or minus $\frac{1}{16}$ in.

Jim Anderson is a framing contractor living in Littleton, Colorado.

Framing Cathedral Ceilings

■ BY BRIAN SALUK

started framing houses years ago, before cathedral ceilings came into fashion. When asked to frame my first cathedral ceiling, I went at it much as I did any other roof. After bracing the walls plumb with leftover 10-ft. 2x4s, my crew set the ridge and the rafters, seemingly without a hitch. It was just another gable roof, only without the ceiling joists. When we finished setting the rafters, it was lunchtime.

I remember biting into my ham-and-cheese sandwich and looking back at the roof. I expected that feeling of satisfaction one gets looking on the results of a good morning's labor. Instead, I got a sinking feeling: The center of the ridge was sagging.

Back in the house, I saw that the weight of the roof pushing out on the walls had actually pulled some of the braces from the floor. Fortunately, it took only a couple of hours to jack the ridge level and pull the walls straight with a come-along. But I was lucky that the only serious loss that day was my uneaten lunch.

Brace the Walls to Resist Roof Thrust

The strength of a typical roof derives from the triangular shape made by the rafters and ceiling joists (see the top photo on p. 100). The ceiling joists tie the exterior walls together, resisting the outward thrust on the exterior walls. Because the joists tie the rafters together as a unit, the rafters carry the downward load on the ridge to the eave walls. Remove the joists, as with a cathedral ceiling, and two things happen. The rafters push out and bow the eave-wall plates, and the ridge becomes load-bearing and sags because it isn't sized to bear a load.

Building cathedral ceilings means finding ways to duplicate the joist's function or eliminating the need for it, both during construction and as part of the permanent structure. Simply put, if you keep the bottoms of

Cathedral ceilings add drama to a room but they provide the builder with the challenge of keeping the walls from spreading during and after construction.

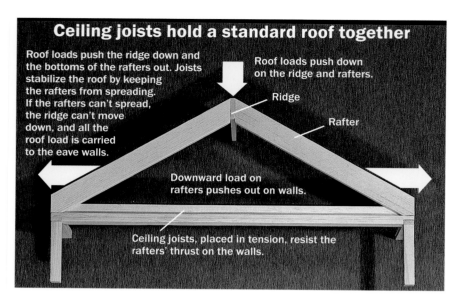

Ceiling joists hold a standard roof together

Roof loads push the ridge down and the bottoms of the rafters out. Joists stabilize the roof by keeping the rafters from spreading. If the rafters can't spread, the ridge can't move down, and all the roof load is carried to the eave walls.

Roof loads push down on the ridge and rafters.

Ridge

Rafter

Downward load on rafters pushes out on walls.

Ceiling joists, placed in tension, resist the rafters' thrust on the walls.

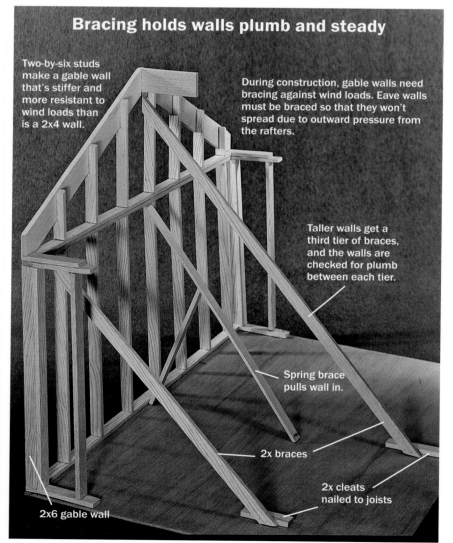

Bracing holds walls plumb and steady

Two-by-six studs make a gable wall that's stiffer and more resistant to wind loads than is a 2x4 wall.

During construction, gable walls need bracing against wind loads. Eave walls must be braced so that they won't spread due to outward pressure from the rafters.

Taller walls get a third tier of braces, and the walls are checked for plumb between each tier.

Spring brace pulls wall in.

2x braces

2x cleats nailed to joists

2x6 gable wall

the rafters from spreading apart or if you keep the ridge from sagging, the roof will be strong and stable.

Proper bracing is the most important consideration during construction. If the walls aren't properly braced, the rafters' thrust will bow the plates, and their weight will sag the ridge. And the wind, blowing against the tall gable-end walls typical of cathedral ceilings, can knock down the whole assembly.

I brace the eave and gable walls plumb at least every 8 ft., with 2x4s half again as long as the wall is high, or 12 ft. for an 8-ft.-high wall. One-story gable walls call for two tiers of braces, one high and one low (see the bottom photo at left). Two-story gable walls get three tiers of braces, and I check the walls for plumb between each tier. I sometimes use 2x6s for the longest braces. The braces are nailed to the tops of studs and to 2-ft.-long 2x4 cleats that are nailed to a floor joist. I use at least two 12d nails at each end of a brace.

Straightening the top plates usually involves pulling the walls in as well as pushing them out. I pull them in with spring braces made from long 2x4s nailed on the flat to the top of the top plates and to the floor at a joist. Jamming a shorter 2x4 under the middle of a spring brace bends it and pulls in on the wall.

T-shaped Posts Support the Ridge

If the ridge of a cathedral ceiling can be kept from sagging, the rafters can't push out the wall plates, and the roof stays put. This is the principle behind the structural-ridge roofs that I will be describing later. With the other types of cathedral ceilings, though, the ridge board isn't load-bearing except during the construction process. Because of this, the ridge board is not sized to take a load and can sag from the weight of the rafters during construction.

To avoid this sagging, I support the ridge with T-shaped posts made by nailing a 2x4 on edge to the center of a 2x6. The T-shape of the post resists buckling under load better than does a single piece of lumber. I space the posts no more than 12 ft. apart and make sure that each one sits over well-supported floor joists. If I have doubts about a post sitting on one joist, I stand the post on a 2x10 or 2x12 laid flat over several joists to spread the load.

Rafters Must Make Room for Insulation

Many framers lay out roofs so that opposing rafters are staggered, making it easy to nail through the ridge into rafter ends. But it's usually best to align opposing rafters in a cathedral ceiling to allow subsequent members to be nailed evenly, instead of at an angle. I keep this in mind when I lay out the mudsills so that floor joists and studs stack under the rafters.

Once I start framing and the customers can finally begin to see the house three-dimensionally, it's common for them to ask if a flat ceiling could become cathedral. If the rafters and ceiling joists aren't already cut, accommodating this request is usually a simple matter of stepping up the original rafter size at least one dimension. For example, I can use 2x8 rafters on a 28-ft.-wide house that has a conventional roof. If the roof were changed to a cathedral style, I'd use at least 2x10 rafters. The reason is two-fold. Extra heft helps to keep the rafters from sagging over time. And without flat ceiling joists, the insulation goes in the roof. The rafters must be wide enough to accommodate the insulation plus space for ventilation.

I have to be selective with rafter material when building cathedral ceilings. The underside of the rafters forms the ceiling plane, so any rafter material with extreme crowns that might show through the finish ceiling gets culled.

The bird's mouths in cathedral rafters have to be cut so that the bottom of the rafter intersects the corner of the top plate. If it doesn't, there would be an area between the ceiling plane and the wall with no nailing for drywall.

Hip and Valley Rafters Can't Hang below Commons and Jacks

Hip and valley rafters are often sized deeper than the rest of the rafters because they carry the combined loads of the jack rafters. Normally, nobody cares if a beefed-up hip or valley rafter hangs down below the other rafters into the attic. But with a cathedral ceiling, a deep rafter would protrude through the finished ceiling. Because of this, if your plans call for an oversize hip or valley rafter, they may have to be made from two smaller members nailed together. If you have any doubts about hip-rafter or valley-

TIP

Be selective with rafter material when building cathedral ceilings. The underside of the rafters forms the ceiling plane, so any rafter material with extreme crowns that might show through the finish ceiling should be culled.

Venting a hip in cathedral ceilings

Hip rafter

One-half-in. deep notches 2 in. or 3 in. long cut in the tops of the jack rafters, where they abut the hip or valley rafter, let air flow from soffit to ridge vent.

Jack rafters

½-in. notches

Working from Scaffolds Speeds Construction

I find it's faster and safer to build cathedral ceilings from scaffolds than to work from ladders. I site-build scaffolds from framing lumber and plywood. Ideally, the scaffold should be high enough so that you can nail the rafters to the ridge and low enough to ease nailing the joists, if any, to the rafters.

The main supports for the scaffolds I build are goalpost-shaped assemblies with 2x4 legs and at least 2x6 horizontal members. I cross-brace these with more 2x4s and space them about 8 ft. apart. Two-by-tens are laid across the goalposts and covered with sheets of plywood. The posts should be high enough to support toeboards and guardrails.

rafter size, consulting an engineer is wise. Alternatively, you could fur the ceiling out to the level of the protruding hip or valley. Finally, ventilation along a hip or valley requires some thought (see the photo on p. 101).

Once all the rafters are up, I usually sheathe the roof. The ridge is still supported with temporary posts, so the roof assembly is strong enough for my men to work on. Sheathing the roof at this point stiffens it and takes the bounce out of the rafters, making it easier to nail the subsequent members to them.

Raising the Ceiling Joists Is the Simplest Cathedral Ceiling

Raising the stable triangle of joists and rafters upward is not much more complex than framing a standard gable roof (see the

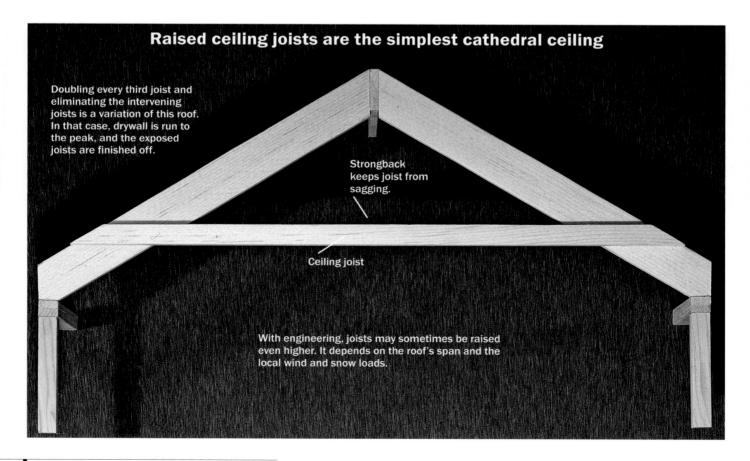

Raised ceiling joists are the simplest cathedral ceiling

Doubling every third joist and eliminating the intervening joists is a variation of this roof. In that case, drywall is run to the peak, and the exposed joists are finished off.

Strongback keeps joist from sagging.

Ceiling joist

With engineering, joists may sometimes be raised even higher. It depends on the roof's span and the local wind and snow loads.

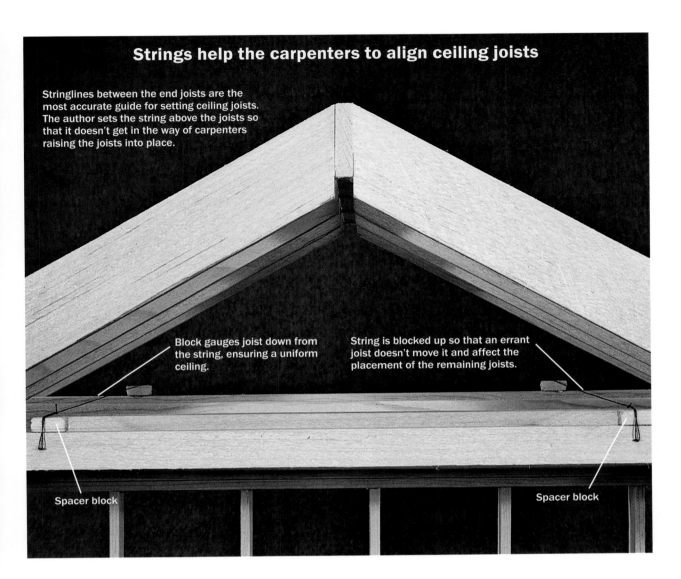

Strings help the carpenters to align ceiling joists

Stringlines between the end joists are the most accurate guide for setting ceiling joists. The author sets the string above the joists so that it doesn't get in the way of carpenters raising the joists into place.

Block gauges joist down from the string, ensuring a uniform ceiling.

String is blocked up so that an errant joist doesn't move it and affect the placement of the remaining joists.

Spacer block

Spacer block

photo on facing page). It's probably the least expensive route, and the mix of angles and flats makes for an interesting ceiling. But if the triangle becomes too small, it can't stabilize the roof. I'll raise these joists about one-third of the distance from the top of the wall to the underside of the ridge. Lower is stronger.

Ceiling joists can often be raised higher than this, but a variety of factors comes into play. The room width, the roof pitch, and the snow load all must be considered. It's wise to consult a structural engineer before raising the joists higher.

I frame this roof much as I would a normal gable roof, starting with the end rafters, the gable walls, and the ridge. After support-

ing the ridge with a T-post, my crew sets the rafters.

After deciding their height, I install the joists. They must be level and in plane with each other. I measure up from the floor and mark the height on both gable walls. A joist is nailed at both ends of the room and checked for level.

I locate the rest of the joists with strings, rather than by snapping chalklines on the underside of the rafters. The rafters are never crowned exactly the same; thus, a chalkline won't be straight, and the ceiling won't be flat. I cut blocks from a piece of scrap and nail them atop the ends of the gable joists. I string a line on each side of the room from these blocks and space the remaining joists down from the lines with other blocks (see the photo on p. 103). The joists don't touch the string, reducing the chance of accidentally pushing it out of line. The strings are set above the joists so that my crew doesn't have to wrestle them over the strings. Variation in joist width isn't usually a problem, particularly if all the stock comes from the same pile of lumber. The joists are nailed to the rafters with at least six 12d nails in each joint. I cut the joists to the roof angle so that there is more wood to nail into than if the joists were square-cut. I cut them just short enough so that they won't touch the roof sheathing. This way, the rafters won't shrink past the joist ends, creating bumps in the roof.

If the span is sizable, I use wider joists. For spans up to 14 ft., 2x6s are fine; beyond that, I increase to 2x8s. If the joists span more than 12 ft., I nail a 2x4 flat to the top of the joists, running perpendicular to the joists and centered in the span. A 2x6 on edge is nailed to the 2x4, creating a strongback. I place the strongback material on top of the joists before installing all of them. Otherwise, I won't be able to get the material up there at all.

A variation on this ceiling is to double the joists on every third rafter pair and leave out the intervening joists. Similar caveats about not raising the joists more than one-third the roof height apply. On this ceiling, the drywall goes all the way to the peak. The doubled joists are exposed, and either drywalled or finished with trim stock.

Scissors Trusses Can Be Site-Built

A scissors truss consists of two opposing rafters braced by two pitched ceiling joists (or truss chords) that resemble lower-slope rafters (see the photo below). The chords cross at the ceiling's peak and continue upward to lap the rafters. This ceiling works well when the customer wants an unbroken

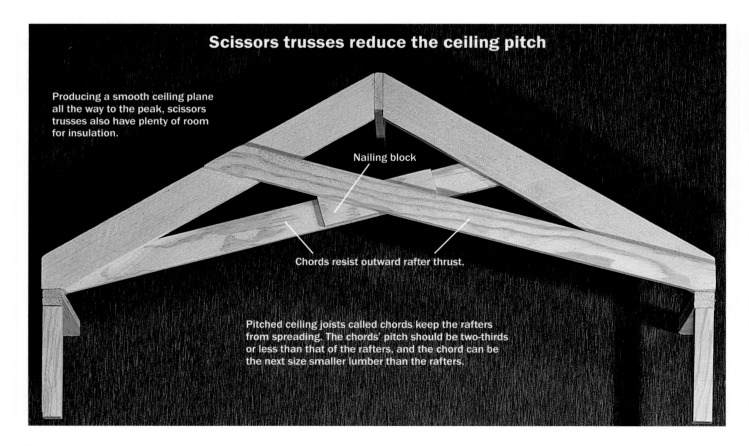

Scissors trusses reduce the ceiling pitch

Producing a smooth ceiling plane all the way to the peak, scissors trusses also have plenty of room for insulation.

Nailing block

Chords resist outward rafter thrust.

Pitched ceiling joists called chords keep the rafters from spreading. The chords' pitch should be two-thirds or less than that of the rafters, and the chord can be the next size smaller lumber than the rafters.

ceiling plane right up to the peak. It's also good if the client wants the ceiling to be a shallower pitch than the roof is.

The chord's pitch shouldn't exceed two-thirds of the rafter's pitch. In other words, if the rafters are a 9-in-12 pitch, the chords should be a 6-in-12 or lower pitch. The steeper the pitch of the chords, the less effective they are at bracing the rafters. I make the chords one size smaller in depth than the rafters.

Framing a scissors-truss roof begins similarly to framing a raised-joist roof. Set the gables and the ridge. Brace the ridge, set the rafters, and partially sheathe the roof. Here, it's especially important to lay out the rafters so that they align at the ridge.

The gable rafters are supported by walls, so there is no need to brace them with chords. The gable-end chords essentially serve as drywall nailers and are nailed to the gable walls. I lay them out just like common rafters, without deducting for a ridge. After nailing up the gable-end chords, I cut the bird's mouth on a piece of chord stock that's long enough to span from the wall to the opposing rafter. I hold this chord stock in place, even with one of the gable-end chords. By marking the chord stock where it laps the opposing rafter, I have the pattern for the rest of the chords.

To line up the chords, I string two lines from the top of the end chords, just as I did with the raised-ceiling-joist roof. The chords are nailed on opposing sides of rafter pairs with six 12d nails per joint. I also toenail them to the wall plate. The chords are lined up on the strings and nailed to the rafter on the far side of the ridge. Where the chords cross, they're the thickness of the rafter apart. I nail a 2-ft. block of the chord material flush with the bottom of one chord and nail the second chord to the block.

Structural ridge beam keeps roof from sagging

Because the ridge carries roof loads to a gable wall, gable-wall framing under the ridge must establish an uninterrupted load path. Headers in this path should be engineered. Use LVL headers, and the manufacturer will usually engineer them for free.

1/2-in. gap for ventilation

Structural ridge doesn't sag under design load, so rafters don't push out on walls.

Three-member structural ridge, often composed of engineered lumber

Continuous 2x6 framing carries load to foundation.

Beam under ridge carries roof load

A variation of a structural ridge, an exposed beam supports the ridge and carries roof loads to the gable walls. Often finish-grade material, this beam calls for careful handling.

Bird's mouths

Exposed beam

Continuous 2x6 framing carries load to foundation.

Design the Ridge as a Beam, and No Joists Are Needed

Another approach to cathedral ceilings is to make the ridge a beam that's stiff enough not to sag under load (see the photo on p. 105). I build this type of roof when a ceiling that climbs cleanly to the peak at the roof pitch is wanted.

A structural ridge creates point loads that must be carried through the gable wall to the foundation with continuous, stacking framing. Headers in this load path need to be sized accordingly, and their studs may need beefing up, too.

I balloon-frame particularly tall gable walls. The studs in balloon-framed gable walls reach from the bottom plate on the first floor to the top plate just below the rafters. Balloon-framing avoids the plates at the various floor levels common to platform-framed walls. Plates can act as a hinge, weakening tall walls. To stop the chimney effect these continuous stud cavities can have in a fire, codes specify fire blocking at least every 8 ft. and where the wall intersects floors and ceilings.

In areas where gable walls are subject to high wind loads, I frame gable walls with continuous 2x6 laminated-strand lumber (LSL) studs. LSL is factory made by shredding lumber and gluing the strands back together. LSL is denser and stiffer than solid-sawn lumber, and it makes for a stronger but more expensive wall.

I avoid large, single-member ridge beams. They're heavy and often must be placed with a crane. I prefer to assemble in place two, three, or even four full-length laminated-veneer lumber (LVL) members that can be lifted by hand. LVLs can span greater distances than standard lumber and are made from material similar to LSL studs. And LVL manufacturers will usually size the beam for you at no extra cost.

Individual ridge members longer than 24 ft. are usually too heavy to lift by hand. In that case, I'll assemble the beam on the ground and lift it with a crane. It's important to build beams straight; once nailed, they're nearly impossible to straighten.

Before nailing together a multimember beam in the air, I set the gable rafters and wall. On 2x6 gable walls, my crew sets the first beam member between the gable rafters just like a ridge board. The subsequent members are cut shorter so that they butt to the inside of the gable rafters. Even after deducting 1½ in. for the gable rafter, the beam has a full 4 in. of bearing. I stagger these shorter members down so that they're about ½ in. lower than the top of the rafters. This method allows air to flow to the ridge vent. After nailing the beam together, I measure, cut, and then install the post under the beam to carry the load downward.

For 2x4 gable walls, all members of the ridge beam must run through the entire width of the wall to gain sufficient bearing. This means that all the beam members have to be placed at the same time as the gable rafters, a trickier operation. Because of this situation and because 2x6 gable walls are stiffer, I rarely build 2x4 gable walls when using a structural ridge.

Show a Finished Beam beneath the Ridge

This roof goes up similarly to the previous example, except that the beam is installed below and supports a standard ridge (see the photo on the facing page). I build this type of roof when the customer wants to show a large finished beam or when the ridge beam is so deep that it would hang below the rafters anyway. In that case, I often put collar ties just below the beam for drywall nailers.

This eliminates the need to drywall and finish that awkward triangular space between the rafters and the side of the beam.

Shorter beams that are light enough to be handled by a couple of carpenters can be installed after the rafters are set. With longer beams, however, especially big single-member beams, it's easier to set the beam first, then build the roof around it.

Again, the first step is building the gable walls and setting the gable rafters. The wall must have a post to support the beam, just as in the structural-ridge type of roof. I cut the gable rafters normally and set the beam within them by hand or by crane.

If this beam is to show, I treat it with care. I hoist it with nylon slings instead of chains, which can mar the surface. And I don't nail temporary braces to the finish face. The nail holes might show, and worse, if the nails rust, they'll deeply stain the beam.

The rafter tops will have bird's-mouth cuts in them that fit over the beam. I don't toenail through the upper seat cut; this usually splits the top of the rafter. Rather, I nail the rafter to the ridge and toenail the ridge to the beam. When laying out this seat cut, I allow for the height of the ridge board plus ¼ in. or so. The rafters don't have to touch the beam because the ridge does. This ¼ in. allows a bit of play that simplifies setting the rafters.

Brian Saluk is a framing contractor from Berlin, Connecticut.

Building Rake Walls

■ BY LARRY HAUN

Most wall layout is quite simple. The process of transferring dimensions from prints to concrete slab or subfloor usually consists of little more than snapping a series of chalklines to form squares and rectangles. On occasion, however, plans will call for a room with a cathedral ceiling that follows the pitch of the roof. Here rafters double as joists, rising upward from an outside wall to the ridge. Gable-end walls in these rooms are called rake walls, and laying one out isn't much more difficult than laying out a regular wall. But being aware of a couple of simple techniques will speed up the process. The methods I discuss here have served me well for the past 40 years.

The location of the bottom 2x plate of a rake wall is laid out on the floor like any other wall. The location of the rake wall's top plate is chalklined out at an angle from the top of the shortest stud. This way, the framer can build the wall without making any further calculations, even though each stud will be a different length. The angle of the top plate is determined by the pitch of the roof.

A Calculated Solution

There are two fairly easy ways of laying out rake walls. The first calls for a pocket calculator, which is used to determine the difference in length between the shortest and longest studs. The shortest stud is normally a standard length, 92¼ in., so once you've established the *difference* in length between shortest and longest, you know the *actual* length of the longest stud. With the heights of both studs established, you'll know the position of the top plate, as well.

To determine the difference in length between the shortest and longest studs in a rake wall, you need to know both the length of the wall and the pitch of the roof. For example, in a house that's 33 ft. wide, a rake wall running to the center of the roof is 16 ft. 6 in. long. With a 6-in-12 roof pitch, multiply 6 by 16 ft. 6 in. (6 in. of rise for every foot of run and 16 ft. 6 in. of run) for a result of 99 in. Add 99 in. to the length of your shortest stud, and you've got the length of your longest stud — 191¼ in.

Now go back to the subfloor to lay out the top plate (see the illustration on p. 110). First, go to the end of the chalkline marking the bottom plate, where the plan indicates the low point of the rake wall. Usually this

Snapping a line. A chalkline can be snapped across the tops of studs and cripples to mark a cutline. Before anything is cut to length, the framers will set the top plate on edge above the line and mark the framing layout on it.

will be at an exterior wall, but check the plans for the exact location of the shortest stuff. Measure up 92¼ in. on the subfloor and mark that point. Next come over 16 ft. 6 in. along the same chalkline to the house's center. Measure up 191¼ in. from there for the long stud and mark that point. Make sure your measurements are perpendicular to the chalkline. Connect the two points with a chalkline, and you've established the location of your top plate. Intermediate studs can now be cut to length without any further calculations.

No Math, No Sweat

Not every good carpenter tackles problems this way, however, and calculators still haven't become commonplace in most tool belts. Another method of laying out rake walls, developed by framers, dispenses with calculation altogether. The trick is to work on a 12-ft. grid and to figure the pitch in feet rather than inches (see the illustration on p. 111).

Let's look at the same problem again: a 6-in-12 pitch and a 16 ft. 6 in. wall. Measure up 92¼ in. from the bottom-plate chalkline at the low end of the rake wall. Mark that point; the height of the short stud hasn't changed. Next, come over 12 ft. along the bottom-plate chalkline and again measure up 92¼ in. perpendicular to the chalkline. Mark this point. So far, all you've done is lay out a rectangle that is 92¼ in. on the short sides and 12 ft. on the long sides.

From the last point, at the 92¼ in. mark, measure straight up in feet whatever the roof pitch is in inches. In this example, because you're working with a 6-in-12 roof pitch, measure up 6 ft. (the rise for a 12-ft. run) and mark that point. Snap a line between this point and the top of your short stud, and you've got your roof pitch. Because your wall is longer than 12 ft., it's necessary to extend this top-plate chalkline several feet. Complete the layout by snapping a chalkline that will represent the outside edge of the longest stud at 16 ft. 6 in. You now have a full-size layout of the rake wall. This process works regardless of the

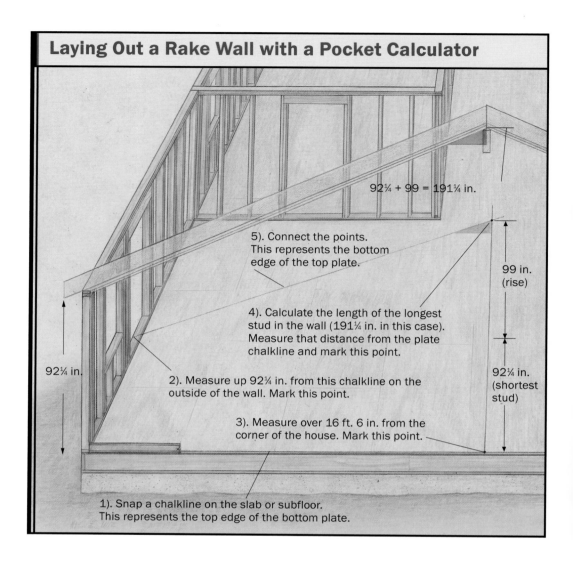

Laying Out a Rake Wall with a Pocket Calculator

92¼ + 99 = 191¼ in.

5). Connect the points. This represents the bottom edge of the top plate.

99 in. (rise)

4). Calculate the length of the longest stud in the wall (191¼ in. in this case). Measure that distance from the plate chalkline and mark this point.

92¼ in. (shortest stud)

92¼ in.

2). Measure up 92¼ in. from this chalkline on the outside of the wall. Mark this point.

3). Measure over 16 ft. 6 in. from the corner of the house. Mark this point.

1). Snap a chalkline on the slab or subfloor. This represents the top edge of the bottom plate.

pitch of the roof or the length of the wall and usually can be completed in just a few minutes.

You may run into a situation where there isn't enough floor space to lay out the rake wall using this method. When that occurs, simply cut the wall length in half and lay out the pitch as a 3-in-6 instead of a 6-in-12. This way, you only need 6 ft. of floor space.

Remember that the lines snapped on the floor show the length of the shortest and longest studs (at their outside edges), the roof pitch, and the length of the wall. The bottom plate goes below the bottom line, and the top plate goes above the top line as the wall is framed.

Framing a Rake Wall

Once you've got the perimeter of your rake wall laid out, mark two bottom plates (you'll see why in a moment) with stud, window, and door locations. Place a stud at every layout mark, letting them extend a little beyond the top-plate chalkline. Nail these studs to one bottom plate, including any trimmer and king studs. Also nail in any headers at this stage. Cripples on top of the headers need to run past the top-plate chalkline, just as the studs do. Next, position the bottom plate so that its top edge is on, but below, the chalkline. Tack it in place with a few 8d nails to make sure it stays straight, and use the extra bottom plate as a layout guide to align the loose top ends of the studs. Then pull a chalkline on the studs

Laying Out a Rake Wall on a 12-ft. Grid

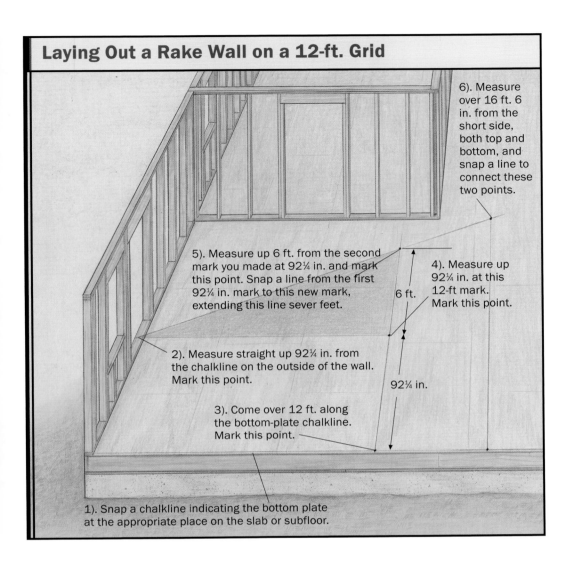

6). Measure over 16 ft. 6 in. from the short side, both top and bottom, and snap a line to connect these two points.

5). Measure up 6 ft. from the second mark you made at 92¼ in. and mark this point. Snap a line from the first 92¼ in. mark to this new mark, extending this line sever feet.

4). Measure up 92¼ in. at this 12-ft mark. Mark this point.

6 ft.

2). Measure straight up 92¼ in. from the chalkline on the outside of the wall. Mark this point.

92¼ in.

3). Come over 12 ft. along the bottom-plate chalkline. Mark this point.

1). Snap a chalkline indicating the bottom plate at the appropriate place on the slab or subfloor.

directly over the roof-pitch line and snap it to mark the studs for length (see the photo on p. 109). Before cutting the studs to length, bring in the piece of lumber that will be your new top plate, place it on the edge directly above the chalkline, mark it for length, and indicate on it where the studs will be nailed once they are cut.

Now it's time to cut the studs to length. If the saw's shoe tilts in the right direction to make the cut, set it at the proper degree for the roof pitch (26½° for a 6-in-12 pitch). If the angles marked on the studs run opposite the direction in which your saw tilts, first cut them square and then make a second cut at the correct angle. The next step is to nail on the top and double plates. Lap the double plate over 3½ in. at the low end to tie the two walls together at the corner.

How Much Precision Is Necessary?

It's been my experience that carpenters often spend too much time on rake walls, trying to build them to extremely fine tolerances. It usually doesn't matter if these walls get built a little high or a little low. With a site-built roof, I actually like to run the rake wall at least 1 in. high so that a good tie can be made between it and the rafter sitting atop it.

Larry Haun is the author of Habitat for Humanity: How to Build a House (2002), published by The Taunton Press, Inc. He lives in Coos Bay, Oregon.

Straightening Framed Walls

■ BY DEREK MCDONALD

As a craftsman, I'm offended when I notice bowed walls and wavy ceilings in newly finished houses. Everyone knows it's tough to find straight, knot-free lumber these days. But bad lumber is not the only cause of bad walls. Extreme weather conditions that strike before the roof is dried in, as well as fluctuations in temperature and humidity afterward, can make even good studs go bad.

The frequency of warped and twisted studs in the average frame house can be reduced if lumber is kept banded and covered until the framers are ready for it. Conscientious framers will also crown moderately bowed studs and cull the worst offenders, setting them aside for use as nailers and blocking. Unfortunately, the supply of skilled labor seems to be dwindling faster than that of straight lumber; so my company maintains a crew of "pickup" carpenters like me who follow behind the framers, straightening studs and flattening walls.

Tolerances Vary from Room to Room

I work for a high-volume framing contractor who builds tract houses in California, so I have to balance my perfectionist tendencies with the pressure to get the job done as efficiently as possible. Keeping this balance requires me to choose which walls are most critical and will thus receive more of my attention. The choice is not difficult; entries and long hallways are more visible than bedrooms, closets, and garages, and are therefore held to a higher standard. More critical are bathrooms—where cabinets and mirrors must lie flat—and kitchens. Because their long rows of cabinets and countertops make flat walls and straight corners essential, kitchens are the most critical rooms of all. For kitchen walls, I allow no more than $\frac{1}{16}$-in. variance from perfectly straight and flat, but I'll accept as much as $\frac{3}{16}$ in. for the garage and the closets.

Efficient Straightening Requires a Good Eye

To minimize stud deflection, I prefer not to begin straightening walls until all roofing tile is in place and until bearing walls are fully loaded. Once I start working, all my measuring is done by eye. My tape measure never leaves the toolbox, and I rarely use a chalk box or dry line.

I use the top and bottom plates as starting points to check the straightness of a ver-

Trust your eye. A visual check gives a good indication of straightness. In most of the cases, when all of the studs fall crisply into line, the wall is acceptable.

tical plane, so my first step is to verify that both ends of each stud are flush with the plates. Any stud that isn't where it's supposed to be gets hammered into position and toenailed. With the starting points in alignment, I give myself a glimpse of the work ahead by sighting down the length of the wall (see the photo above) and visually lining up the studs. A quick glance such as

this one lets me know what gross irregularities are lurking, and when all the studs line up like soldiers, I know there's a good chance I can move on to the next wall.

Unless every stud lines up perfectly, the next step is to find out where the deviants are. This step requires a long straightedge. Any perfectly straight piece of wood or steel will do, but because I believe a lightly armed

Desperate Measures

On those rare occasions when an offending stud cannot easily be planed, shimmed, or simply removed, more elaborate solutions are called for. "Strong-backing" (photo above) is one technique to force a severely bowed (more than ⅜ in.) stud back into alignment and keep it there. A bowed corner stud (photo right) must be temporarily cut loose and then wedged out from the corner before it can be planed straight.

carpenter is an efficient one, I use the same 8-ft. box level that I use for plumbing walls. I've also found that the smooth surface of my box level is much kinder to my fingers after a day of continuous handling than the rough edges of wood or the sharp edges of steel.

Repairs Are Noted on Stud Face

I prefer to straighten one wall at a time: eye-balling, making note of problems, and performing necessary surgery before moving on to the next wall. Starting in a corner and working my way out, I place the straight-edge vertically against each stud and trust my eye to judge the amount of correction needed, and where (see the photo below). Using a simple shorthand we've devised, I mark the remedy directly on the face of each offending stud using a lumber crayon. If the stud bows outward, I squiggle an

A little daylight is a bad, bad thing. Using a straightedge that runs from top plate to bottom plate, the author can easily determine how much a stud deviates from the ideal. Because it's part of a highly visible hallway, this stud will need a shim.

A prescription for change. The author checks every stud with a straightedge and marks the remedies on the stud faces as he goes. An S-shaped squiggle indicates that the stud needs to be planed. Hash marks indicate the number of shims needed.

Planing begins at the midpoint. To straighten a bowed stud without measuring, the author starts with a foot-long pass in the middle and overlaps with increasingly longer passes.

S-shape over the area that needs to be planed. If the stud bows inward, I make one or more hash marks in the center of the bow to indicate the number of cardboard furring strips I estimate I'll need to fill in the gap (see the photo at left above).

If I find a stud that needs more than ⅜ in. of planing or furring, I put a big X on the face. This note reminds me to come back later with a reciprocating saw, cut the nails that anchor the stud to the plates, and replace it. Sometimes it's difficult to replace one of these bad studs—it could be part of a complicated framing scheme, or maybe the electrician has beaten me to the job and run wires through the walls. In this case, we straighten the stud using a technique we call strong-backing.

Strong-backing is accomplished by notching the offending stud at midpoint (on the face that bows outward) to let in a 2x4 or 2x6 on the flat. We cut a block to fit between the two studs that flank the bad one; then we nail one end to one of the flanking studs and use the block as a lever to draw the of-

fender back into the plane of the wall. When the offender has been reformed, we nail the free end to the side of the other flanking stud (see the top photo on the facing page).

Plane First, Ask Questions Later

After each stud has been checked with a straightedge, I use my planer to take off high spots. Unless I know that a knot high or low on the stud is causing the bow, I begin planing at the midpoint of the stud. Starting with a foot-long pass, I overlap with increasingly longer passes until I have planed most of the stud's length (see the photo at right above). The severity of the

How do you spell relief? Available in bundles of 50, precut cardboard shims make quick work of a tedious job.

from the adjoining wall's corner stud to allow room for the planer (see the bottom left photo on p. 114). If planing is the only solution, I first drive a small wooden wedge between the afflicted stud and the stud to which it is nailed. This step allows room to slide my reciprocating saw's blade between the two studs to cut the nails holding them together. Then I force the corner stud out by driving two thick wedges between the studs, one about 2 ft. from each end. After planing the bow, I remove the wedges and renail the stud.

Precut Shims Make Life Worth Living Again

After I've planed the high spots, I then shim the low spots. Shimming studs used to be a tedious process of trial and error, but that changed a few years ago when we started buying precut cardboard shim stock (see the photo at left above). I'm told there are different varieties of precut shims available now; the ones we've used are 45-in.-long, $\frac{1}{16}$-in.-thick cardboard strips that come bundled in groups of 50.

bow determines the number of passes. When I think I've removed enough material, I get the straightedge and check my work.

Planing is a straightforward procedure unless the offender is a corner stud. An outwardly bowed corner stud must either be replaced or temporarily wedged far enough

The procedure I use for shimming is similar to the one I use for planing. Often, a single shim is sufficient. But if the bow is a pronounced one, I start by laying down a short (1 ft. or 2 ft. long) strip over the midpoint of the bow. Then I work outward from the center of the bow, overlapping (by various amounts) successively longer strips to achieve a blending effect. I fasten the shim stock to the studs using a hammer tacker loaded with ⅜-in. staples (see the photo at left).

An efficient shimming operation. Duct tape and a scrap piece of drain pipe create a handy quiver to ensure that the cardboard shim stock is always within the author's reach.

After I've planed and shimmed all the studs in the wall, I need to check the plane of the entire wall. At this time, I place the straightedge horizontally across the studs, at various points up and down the wall, to see how the framing surfaces flow together (see the photo at right). If adjacent studs vary from plane more than the fraction of an inch I allowed when I was straightening individual studs, that means I still have to do a bit of planing or furring to fine-tune the wall.

Don't Plane a Truss without Prior Approval

Most of my effort goes toward straightening walls, but I don't ignore ceilings. I follow essentially the same procedure for ceilings as I do for the least critical walls. Large rooms can be a problem, though, because an 8-ft. straightedge is too short to give a true idea of straightness. So when my eye picks out a serious irregularity, I pull a dry line from one end of the suspect framing member to the other. An upward bow is easily shimmed to meet the line. A downward bow is another story.

If the framing members were solid-sawn joists, I could snap a chalkline on the side of the joist and plane to the line. Unfortunately, I work with trusses. Although the engineer who designs our trusses will allow me to plane up to ¼ in. off the bottom chord, he prefers that I "paper down when feasible." What he means is that rather than plane up to the line, I should shim down to the low point. Because this procedure lowers the surface of the truss in question beneath that of its neighbors, I then have to draw my straightedge across the chords and shim the adjacent framing surfaces enough to feather out the differences.

Use Your Illusion

Whether the subject is walls or ceilings, it's important to keep in mind that I'm hardly ever trying to create perfectly flat surfaces. In most cases, my goal is to create the illusion of perfection; I do it by straightening

Sources

Fortifiber Co.®
55 Starkey Ave.
Attleboro, MA 02703
(800) 343-3972
www.fortifiber.com
pre-cut shims

Checking the plane of the wall. After the offending studs have been planed and shimmed for vertical straightness, the author then checks across the studs to see how they line up horizontally.

and aligning, as much as the laws of physics and time allow, and by blending and creating smooth transitions where they do not exist. Consider, for example, a long wall in which 11 of 14 studs have a slight but consistent inward bow. By planing the three straight studs to imitate the shape of the others, I can reach a compromise between aesthetics and economics. The other option—furring all 11 bowed studs—would take twice as much time, and no one would know it but me.

*When he's not surfing the pipeline, **Derek McDonald** works as a carpenter for HnR Framing Systems Inc. in Poway, California.*

Balloon-Framing a Rake Wall

■ BY SEAN SHEEHAN

Here in Montana, the wind is something you can count on. The broad mountain valleys that grace this state are, among other things, nature's wind tunnels (the high plains are called windswept for a good reason). A builder must contend with the wind during all phases of a project, and any building should be designed with the wind in mind.

One technique that our crew uses to increase the wing resistance of a rake wall (a wall whose top plate follows the incline of the roof) is balloon-framing. Wherever we can, we extend the rake-wall studs all the way from the floor to the roofline rather than frame a conventional wall and stand a truss on it or fill in above the wall with gable-end studs.

Balloon- vs. Platform-Framing

In balloon-framing, studs run continuously from foundation to roof. The second floor, if there is one, hangs from the studs. In platform-framing, which evolved from balloon-framing as a safer and more efficient form of construction, the second floor is built on top of the first-floor walls. Then the second-floor walls are framed on top of the platform (hence the name). With this system the top plates of the first-floor walls serve as firestops; in balloon-framing, firestops have to be added. Platform-framing also requires shorter studs, which are easier to handle, and provides a safe platform (the second floor) on which to work, rather than requiring the carpenter to build walls 16 ft. in the air.

Nonetheless, there are times when balloon-framing makes sense. I consider it essential when building a tall, window-filled rake wall in a home with high cathedral ceilings. Even when sheathed with plywood, the platform-framed version of this wall can literally billow in the wind. The top plates that divide a platform-framed wall from the rake-wall studs above it create a break line. When the wind pushes against such an arrangement and there is no interior structure (such as a second floor or a partition wall) to resist it, the wall flexes at the break line.

The structural integrity of balloon-framing can be undermined by careless placement of windows and doors. We try to ensure that studs in the center third of a rake wall are left intact. If this is impossible, we double up king studs, or sometimes triple-stud the center of a wall if there are windows on both sides of center. The object is a stiffer wall, so we leave enough of the studs in one piece to achieve this goal.

We use two basic methods to balloon-frame a rake wall. If we have the space, we build it on the first-floor deck. We usually divide a peaked wall into two wedge-shaped walls and nail them together after the walls are up. This provides more workspace on the deck and puts a double stud in the center that runs to the peak. If we don't have room on the deck, then we build the wall in place, or "in the air," as we call it.

First, the Math

Usually, the eave height and the length of the wall are known, and I have to determine the peak height, the length of the top plate, and the length of each stud. The peak height is determined by the pitch of the roof we're building. Let's assume a 6-in-12 pitch, a wall length of 12 ft., and an eave height of 8 ft. Over 12 ft., a 6-in-12 pitch will rise 6 ft. Add 6 ft. to the height of the eave for a peak height of 14 ft. To find the length of the top plate, it's helpful to think of the wall as a right triangle on top of a rectangle (see the bottom illustration on p. 120). The rectangle is 12 ft. by 8 ft. (the length of the wall by the height at the eave), and the right triangle is 6 ft. high and 12 ft. long with an unknown hypotenuse (the top plate). I use the Pythagorean theorem ($a^2 + b^2 = c^2$) to find the length of the top plate.

In this case, $a = 6$ (the length of one leg) and $b = 12$ (the length of the other leg).

When there isn't room on the deck, Sheehan's crew builds rake walls "in the air," standing up the basic frame, then filling in the studs. After laying out the bottom plate, they use a plumb bob to transfer the layout to the top plate, provided the wind isn't blowing too hard.

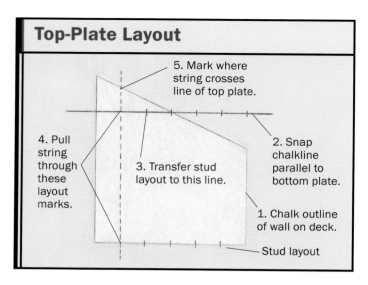

Top-Plate Layout

5. Mark where string crosses line of top plate.

4. Pull string through these layout marks.

3. Transfer stud layout to this line.

2. Snap chalkline parallel to bottom plate.

1. Chalk outline of wall on deck.

Stud layout

Plugging these numbers into the formula, you'll find that c^2 must be equal to 180. Now all you need is to find the square root of 180, which is 13.416 ft., or 13 ft. 5 in.

On the Deck

Once I have the length of the top and bottom plates and the height of the wall at both ends, I chalkline a full-scale pattern of the wall on the deck, being careful to keep the pattern square.

To mark the stud locations on the top plate, another carpenter and I snap a line parallel to the bottom plate that crosses the top plate somewhere near the middle (see the illustration above). Next we transfer the bottom plate layout to this line. Then we pull a string through the stud layout of both the bottom plate and this line. We mark the points where the string crosses the line of the top plate.

Once the layout is accurately transferred to the top plate, it's a simple matter to measure stud lengths. We refer to the measurement as being to the "long side" or the "short side" to avoid confusion, and if we're building more than one wall from the pattern, we write the measurements on the deck below each stud.

In the Air

When there is no deck on which to lay out the wall, we take a different approach. If the wall is short enough that the top plate can be cut from a single piece of lumber, we simply cut the plates and the end studs, nail these together, and erect this frame. Once the frame is up and braced plumb, we lay our studs on the bottom plate. If the wind isn't blowing, the layout can be transferred to the top plate with a plumb bob (see the photo on p. 119).

If the wind is blowing, we nail a 2x4 horizontally across the outside of the frame, level with the top of the shortest stud. We then transfer the stud layout onto this. Next we stretch a string from the bottom plate layout through the layout on the 2x4 to the top plate, and mark where the string crosses the top plate. If we don't trust the straightness of the top plate (and we never do), we pull a string along its top and use a temporary stud to correct the bow.

If the wall is long enough to require a two- or three-piece top plate, the wall can be equally divided. The lengths of the studs that will stand beneath the breaks in the top plate can be determined easily with a little math.

The Concept

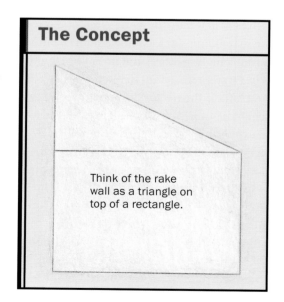

Think of the rake wall as a triangle on top of a rectangle.

Let's return to the hypothetical wall: The length is 12 ft., the shortest stud is 8 ft., the longest stud is 14 ft., and the top plate is 13 ft. 5 in. If we were to break the top plate into two equal pieces 6 ft. 8½ in. long, the length of the stud that would stand under this break in the plate would be equal to half the difference between the length of the shortest and the longest stud, plus the length of the shortest stud, or 11 ft. Again, it helps to use the triangle/rectangle analogy. Simply put, if you cut the triangle in half, the legs will also be cut in half (see the illustration at right). This works with any division.

When this method is used, the wall usually ends up with an extra stud in the center because the layout almost never coincides with the exact center of the wall. Sometimes the center stud interferes with the installation of another stud, but still doesn't fall on the layout. In this case, we simply add another stud onto the side of the center stud closest to the layout. Keep in mind that if you want the break to fall in the center of the studs, the measurement you arrive at mathematically will be to the center of the angled cut at the top of the stud. This is the only time we deal with a measurement that is neither the "long side" nor the "short side."

Opposite sides of a peaked wall should be identical, and when building "in the air," measurements can be transferred from the top plate on one side to the top plate of the other. If things start coming out "a little off," find out why. Geometry is an exact science, and if the studs that fit on one side are suddenly ¼ in. too long on the other, resist the temptation to just squeeze them in, or push them over and figure it's close enough. Chances are good that ¼ in. isn't nearly close enough.

It's very important to maintain close tolerances when balloon-framing. Particularly on steep pitches, an error in stud length of ⅛ in. can cause a considerable bow in the top plate. This is also true with regard to placing studs on center. And to a lesser

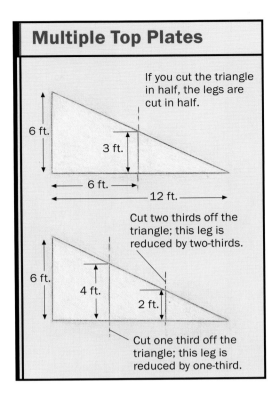

Multiple Top Plates

6 ft.

3 ft.

6 ft.

12 ft.

If you cut the triangle in half, the legs are cut in half.

Cut two thirds off the triangle; this leg is reduced by two-thirds.

6 ft.

4 ft.

2 ft.

Cut one third off the triangle; this leg is reduced by one-third.

extent, it holds true with top plate length. An error of ½ in. can really throw things out of whack. Double-check your math to be sure the figures are right. Once the wall is up, we usually tack the bottom plate in a few places, brace it, and immediately plumb it. When the ends are plumb, we run a quick check on each stud with a 5-ft. level.

Finally, when the wall is permanently nailed and braced, we snap a line the length of the wall at 8 ft. from the floor to serve as an installation reference for the fire blocking. In the event of a fire, this will prevent a wall cavity from behaving like a chimney and increasing both the rate of spread and intensity of the conflagration. We position the blocks in an alternate pattern—one above the line, the next below, so we can nail through the studs and into the blocks. There is a danger of bowing the studs with over-dimension blocks, so here again, we maintain a high standard of accuracy.

Sean Sheehan is a builder in Basin, Montana.

Framing Walls

■ BY SCOTT MCBRIDE

I've heard a lot in recent years about the speed and the efficiency of California framers, but I find it hard to imagine anyone faster than the Italian-American carpenters who taught me to frame walls in the suburbs north of New York City. These men worked with an extraordinary economy of motion.

I want to discuss wall framing in general and, more specifically, to point out some of the methods and tricks I learned while working with New York carpenters. Even though some of these framing methods differ from those practiced elsewhere in the country, they have worked well for me, and I think they can work for anyone who wants to be more efficient on the job.

Carpentry has a vocabulary all its own. *Stud, jack,* and *header* all have meanings outside the carpentry world, but to a framing crew these terms have specific definitions as components of a wall. If you are confused by a sentence that reads, "Toenail the king stud to the bottom plate," then you should familiarize yourself with the illustration on p. 125.

Snapping Chalklines

The first step in any wall-framing method is snapping chalklines on the plywood deck to indicate the locations of the various walls. Wall locations will be shown on the plans. First, I snap lines for all the exterior perimeter walls. If I'm building 2x6 exterior walls—which I usually am these days—I use a 2x6 block to gauge a mark 5½ in. in from the edge of the deck at each end of each wall. To position the block, I sight down to the corner of the foundation or of the story below, aligning the outside edge of the block with this vertical line of sight (see the photo on p. 124). You can't depend on the rim joist (called the box beam in New York) for registering the block because the rim joist is often warped out of plumb. Staying in line with the true corner is desirable, even if it means a bump in the sheathing at floor level. Otherwise the building tends to grow as it goes up, causing inconsistencies in the span that can complicate the roof framing.

After making a mark on all the corners of the deck at 5½ in., I connect the pencil marks with chalklines. I anchor the end of my chalkline with an awl tapped into the deck. When all the exterior walls are snapped out, I move on to the interior partitions, taking measurements from the plans

Nailing the walls together. After all the layout and cutting is finished, the wall components are nailed together. The author nails the doubler to the top plate before the wall is assembled. This then requires that the tops of the studs be toenailed to the plate, instead of through-nailed as in other methods. The pull-out strength of a toenail is greater than that of a through-nail into end grain.

2x6 template. A 2x6 block is used to mark an exterior wall's width on the plywood deck. The author sights down to the floor below to make up for possible irregularities in the alignment of the floor joists.

and transcribing the lines onto the deck. I snap only one line for each wall and scrawl big Xs on the deck with my lumber crayon. The X indicates the side of the line where the wall goes. If there are 2x6 interior partitions as well as ones made of 2x4s, I indicate with my crayon which partitions are which.

Plating the Walls

Plating is the process of cutting to length the bottom and top plates of the walls and temporarily stacking them on the deck (see the photo on the facing page). They can then be marked up to indicate where the various studs and headers will get nailed. In essence, I temporarily put all of the walls in place without the studs in them. My method of framing differs a little from some others in that I cut the doublers now and stack them on top of the other two plates for a three-layer package. Later I'll explain why I do this.

Before cutting any lumber, I think a little about the order in which I want to raise the walls because this sequence determines how the corners of the walls should overlap. Where walls intersect, one wall runs through the intersection. This is called the bywall. The other wall ends at the intersection. This is called the butt wall.

Bywalls have bottom and top plates of the same length that run through the wall intersections. The doubler of a bywall is shorter than the top and bottom plates by the width of the intersecting wall's plates (see the illustration on the facing page). This allows the doubler from the intersecting butt wall to lap the top plate of the bywall. Nailing through the doubler at the lapped corner into the top plate of the intersecting wall holds the walls together.

It is a good idea to cull through your lumber and save your straightest pieces for the longest top plates and doublers. I use the next-best stuff for the bottom plates, which are easier to straighten by nailing to the subfloor. The crooked stuff I cut up for short walls.

There are a couple of things to keep in mind when you are cutting to length the plates and the doublers. Butt joints in the bottom plate can occur almost anywhere. Splices in the top plate—the middle layer—should be offset as much as possible from adjoining walls and beam pockets. Here's why: The integrity of the top-plate assembly —the top plate and the doubler nailed together—depends on having well-staggered joints. An interruption of the doubler is inevitable at wall intersections and beam pockets, so keeping the joints in the middle layer away from these points will maintain good overlap and avoid a weak spot. Splices in the doubler should be kept away from splices in the top plate by at least 4 ft.

If two walls cross each other, you'll have to let one of them run through the intersection and separate the other into two butt walls. The butt-wall doublers can split the overlap, with a joint in the middle of the bywall. Another option is to let one of the butt walls overlap in a full conventional tee. The other butt wall gets no overlap, but instead it is tied to the intersection with a sheet-metal plate on top of the doublers after raising the wall.

Plated and detailed. Information written on the wall plates and the girders defines how the walls are put together. The author also lays out the second-floor joists or roof rafters before assembling the walls. Different-colored ink is used to denote a change in stud length. (Penciled guidelines were drawn on the lumber only for the sake of neatness in this article. It is not common practice for the author.)

The Parts of a Wall

Carpentry has a vocabulary all its own. There is a specific name for every component of a framed wall.

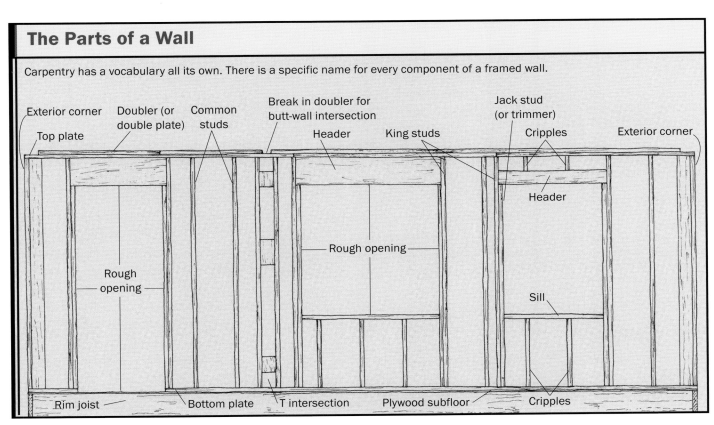

To commence plating, the bottom plates are toenailed to the deck on the chalkline, using 8d common nails about every 8 ft.— just enough to hold them in position. The top plates—the middle layers—are then temporarily toenailed to the bottom plates. Finally, I lay down the doublers—the third layer—over the top plates, but instead of tacking them temporarily, I nail them home with 10d common nails staggered 24-in. o. c. I use 10ds here instead of longer nails because the 10ds won't penetrate the bottom plates.

Remember, at the corners where the walls meet, the orientation of the butt joints is reversed, creating the overlap in the doublers that will ultimately lock the walls together. I don't nail the overlap now because I'll have to separate the walls later.

Detailing the Plates and the Doublers

When all the plates are laid down and held together, and the doublers are nailed in place, I'm ready to mark them up, or detail them, with the information my crew and I will need to frame the walls. The first information recorded on the doublers is the width of the door and window rough openings in the exterior walls. The rough-opening marks I make on the top of the doubler are discreet, only about 1½ in. long. I'm saving most of that surface for a later step in the layout.

If windows or doors are shown on the plans dimensioned to centerlines, I measure from the outside corners and mark the centerlines on the outer edge of the doubler. Then I divide the rough-opening dimension of the door or window in half. For example, if the width of the rough opening for a pair of French doors is 6 ft. 4 in., I'll align 3 ft. 2 in. on my tape with the centerline, then mark lines at 0 and 6 ft. 4 in. To check my arithmetic, I turn my tape around end for end. The center should still be at 3 ft. 2 in.

I make a V to indicate the rough-opening side of each line (see the photo on p. 125).

Rough openings for interior doors are marked the same on the interior-wall doublers as for exterior doors, but the plans will usually call out the size of the finished door rather than a rough opening. To find the rough opening of a door, I add 2 in. to the width. This allows for a ¾-in. thick jamb and a ¼-in. shim space on both sides.

After locating a rough opening on the doubler, find the length of its header. Openings of less than 6 ft. will require one jack stud, or trimmer, on each side of the opening to support the header. Each jack stud is 1½ in. thick, so the header needs to be 3 in. longer than the width of the opening. (Because of variations in the actual thickness of 2x stock—studs can vary in thickness from 1⅜ in. to 1⅝ in.—it is a good idea to measure the lumber you're working with, then do your addition.) Headers over 6 ft. long require double jack studs on each side. That means the length of the header must be 4 times 1½ in., or 6 in., longer than the width of the rough opening.

I use a 2x block as a template to mark the jack locations on the outside of the rough-opening marks. I square the outermost mark down across the stacked edges of the three layers of 2x. This line indicates the end of the header and the inboard face of the king stud. The king stud is the full-length stud to which the jack stud is nailed. On the edges of the top and bottom plates, I show the king stud with an X and the jack stud with an O. For double jacks I use OO. After repeating the process on the other side of the opening, I measure between the outermost marks on the top of the doubler to verify the header length I arrived at earlier by arithmetic. And finally, I write the length of the header on the doubler.

Window headers are marked out the same way as for doors. As far as windowsills and bottom cripples are concerned, I usually come back to them after the walls are up. They aren't needed for structural reasons, and I'm usually in a big hurry to finish the framing and get the roof on. But if I'm going to sheathe the exterior walls before they are tipped into place, I frame below the windows as I go. In that case I'll write the height of the window rough opening on the doubler as well as the width.

I think presheathing pays if you can have the plywood joint even with the bottom of the wall. But some builders, architects, and inspectors require that the plywood joints be offset from the floor elevation to tie the stories together. You can still presheathe in that case by letting the sheets hang over the bottom plate, but I think it becomes more trouble than it's worth. It's usually more economical to let the least skilled members of the crew hang plywood after the walls have been raised.

As soon as I've finished determining all the header sizes, I make a cutlist and give it to a person on the crew who can then get busy making headers while I finish the layout.

Detailing the Doubler

After marking the rough openings on the edges of the top plates and the doubler, the focus shifts back to the top face of the doubler. It's time to lay out the structure that will eventually sit on top of the wall you're about to build. There are very logical reasons to do all this layout now. First, by doing it now, you won't have to spend a lot of time working off a stepladder or walking the plate after the walls are up and the doublers are 8 ft. in the air. The work will already be done. Second, it is easier to align the studs in the wall you're currently building with the loads coming down from above. This is called stacking, and I'll discuss it further later in the article.

The structure that sits on top of the doubler may be either a floor or a roof. In either case I start by locating the principle members —girders in the case of floors, ridges in the case of a roof. I mark their bearing positions on the doublers. Then I measure their actual

Layout trick. A flexible wind-up tape is used for layout. Hold a pencil against the tape and swing it across the plate to make marks. The farther the tape is away from the end of the plate, the straighter the lines will be.

lengths, cut the members, and set them on the doublers. I can now lay out the spacing for the joists or the rafters on the principle beams at the same time I put the corresponding layout on the walls.

To ensure that the principal member is positioned correctly when it's eventually raised, I make a directional notation on the beam, such as north end, or driveway side. With the principal members in position, the first joists or rafters I locate are specials, such as stairway trimmers, dormer trimmers, and joists under partitions.

When all the specials have been marked, I lay out the commons. These are individual, full-length framing members (either joists or rafters in this case). The standard spacing is 16 in. o. c., but 12 in. and 24 in. are not uncommon. You want to minimize the cutting of your plywood, so the spacing of commons should result in 8 ft. landing in the middle of a framing member. Assuming 16-in. centers, I hook my tape on the end of the doubler and tick off 15¼, 31¼, 47¼, etc. As an alternative, you can tick off the first mark at 15¼ and then measure the remaining marks from there on exact 16-in. centers.

You can square the tick marks across the doubler with a square or use this trick: Clamp your pencil point against your tape at the given spacing by pinching them together between your thumb and fingers. Swing an arc across the plate (see the photo on p. 127), move your pencil to the next point, repeat, and so on. The error caused by the curvature of the line is negligible, and it diminishes as you move outward. This trick works better with a flexible wind-up tape than with the stiffer, spring-return tape.

By now you're probably wondering if I'm ever going to start nailing the walls together. Be patient, we're almost ready.

Stacking Studs

The spacing for the common studs in the walls is derived from the joist or rafter spacing in the structure that sits above. If joist or rafter spacing is the same as the stud spacing, both 16 in. o. c., for example, I simply extend the layout mark on the top of the doubler down across the edges of the plates. Aligning the framing members like this is called stacking. But if you have, say, joists on 12-in. centers and studs on 16-in. centers, every fourth joist should stack over every third stud. Stacking wherever possible helps to prevent deflection of the top plate, although it could be argued that the presence of sheathing and band joists makes such deflection unlikely. Stacking does facilitate the running of plumbing pipes as well as heating pipes or HVAC ductwork.

And on exterior walls, stacking studs from one story to the next makes installation of plywood sheathing more efficient. To support a special joist, such as a double 2x trimmer, I square the layout mark on the

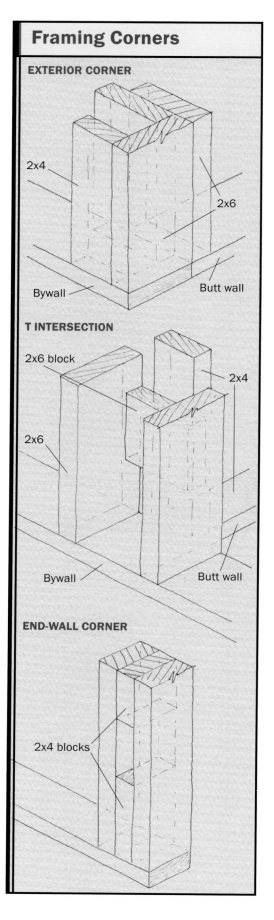

Framing Corners

EXTERIOR CORNER

2x4

2x6

Bywall

Butt wall

T INTERSECTION

2x6 block

2x4

2x6

Bywall

Butt wall

END-WALL CORNER

2x4 blocks

doubler down across the edges of the plates and indicate a special double stud.

Over door-header locations, I extend my pencil marks for the cripple-stud spacing across the edge of the doubler and the top plate, but I stop short of the bottom plate. Instead of marking an X here, I mark a C on the correct side of the line. This will show the carpenters where to put the cripple studs above the door header. Of course, this step is unnecessary if the header sits tight against the top plate. At window headers I extend the mark across the bottom plate as well, writing C for cripple.

The studs in nonbearing partitions running perpendicular to the joists should also stack, although it's not as crucial as for bearing walls. (A nonbearing partition is a wall that doesn't support a load.) For partitions running parallel to the joists, the placement of the common studs is discretionary. They can be laid out from either end of the wall.

Building Corners

With the stud layout completed, there are only a few more details that need to be mopped up before nailing the walls together. At the end of the exterior bywalls I write CORNER, which means a U-shaped corner unit made up of two 2x6s and one 2x4. This corner design permits easy access for fiberglass insulation (see the illustration on the facing page).

Another step in the final layout is to mark out the studs that go at the end of each butt wall where they intersect a bywall. These inside corners provide nailing for drywall and baseboard and, for that matter, any other type of finish trim that might end in a corner.

Some carpenters preassemble channels to back up these T-shaped intersections. I find it easier to space a pair of studs in the bywall, separated by the flat width of a block. I add the blocks after the walls are raised: one in the middle for 8-ft. walls, two or more for taller walls. By using 2x6 blocks behind 2x4 partitions, and 2x8 blocks behind 2x6 parti-

tions, I get a 1-in. space on both sides between the partition and the bywall studs. This provides access for insulation. It also makes nailing drywall and baseboard easier because you don't have to angle the nail as much to catch the corner stud (see the center illustration on the facing page).

Corner posts for interior 2x4 partitions are made up of intermittent blocks that are sandwiched between full-length studs. This type of corner can also be used at the end of peninsular walls (see the bottom illustration on the facing page). Write B to indicate the blocking.

The final layout step is to number each wall for identification and to indicate the raising sequence. As a convention, I write the number on the left end of the doubler as I look down on it. I then write the same number in front of it on the deck in heavy crayon. These steps help prevent the wall from being installed backward, which is easy to do. I put a slash under the 6 and the 9 to tell them apart. If there are different stud lengths within a story, I write the appropriate length next to the raising-sequence number that has been assigned to each wall. It's not a bad idea to use a different-colored crayon or marker to indicate different non-standard stud lengths. For example, if I'm writing everything else out in black crayon, I use a red crayon to make the exceptions easy to spot.

Nailing the Walls Together

When the layout detailing is complete, the temporary toenails are removed from the bottom plate only. Each wall is now represented by a separate package containing the bottom plate, the top plate, and the doubler. I stack these packages in an out-of-the-way place on the deck, along with the headers, the corner units, and the principal beams for the structure above. Studs should be leaned against the edge of the deck where they can be reached, but not stacked on the

Headers and king studs. Tipping the nailed-together doubler and top plate upside down on the deck makes it easy to toenail the header and attach the king stud.

Scribing the jacks. By holding a stud alongside the king stud and against the underside of the header, the jacks can be scribed without measuring. Visible on the bottom plate, half hidden by the carpenter's hand, is a galvanized plate nailed over joints in the plate.

deck. The fastest and most accurate way to mass-produce nonstandard studs is with an improvised double-end cutoff arrangement. Nail two chopsaws or slidesaws to a bench at just the right distance apart. Two operators working together lift a stud onto the beds and cut off both ends. This method squares up both ends of the studs and cuts them to length.

When I'm nailing walls together, I usually start with one of the longer exterior walls. I lay the plate package on the deck, parallel to its designated location and pulled back from the edge of the deck by a little more than the length of the studs. You don't want to crowd yourself. I pull out the nails that hold the bottom plate to the top-plate assembly and spread the plates, moving the bottom plate close to the edge of the deck. I'm real careful not to turn the plate end for end.

I find the wall's headers and carry them over to their locations. If the header sits tightly against the top plate, I flip the top-plate assembly upside down and toenail the header down into the underside of the top plate. Then I stand a king stud upside down on the plate and through-nail it to the end of the header with 16d sinkers or 10d commons. I throw a few toenails through the king stud down into the plate as well (see the photo on the facing page). Now I roll the assembly down flat on the deck.

Some people precut all their jacks, but I like to make them as I nail the walls together. It's simple and fast: I take a common stud and lay it against the king stud, one end butted tightly against the header. Then I strike a line across the bottom end of the king stud onto the jack (see the photo on p. 123) and cut carefully, just removing the pencil line. I nail the jack to the king stud in a staggered pattern, 16 in. o. c. This method of cutting jacks in situ compensates for the variations in header width. The short cutoffs will be used up quickly for blocking.

If the header is offset from the top plate by cripple studs, the wall-framing procedure is substantially the same, except that it's all done flat on the deck, toenailing cripples to the top plate and then to the header (see the photo on p. 125).

Toenailing the Studs

Because the top plate and the doubler are nailed together beforehand, the tops of the studs must be toenailed in place rather than through-nailed. Toenailing requires more skill than through-nailing; it might take a beginner a little longer to learn, but it's not as if it's something he won't have to learn eventually. And toenailing is stronger than through-nailing because it penetrates across the grain. As the walls are jockeyed around on the deck and moved into position to be raised, the bottom plates, which are through-nailed, loosen easily while the toenailed tops hold firm.

If you'd rather not toenail, or if you're using air nailers, which make toenailing difficult, you can tack the doubler to the top plate temporarily for layout purposes. Then pull the doubler off to through-nail the tops of the studs. And finally, nail the doubler back in place using an index mark to ascertain its correct position. Toenailing is the method I was taught years ago, and it's what I'm most comfortable with, so that's the method I'll describe.

When the headers and their jacks and king studs have been nailed in place, I stock the wall with common studs. One end of each stud rests on the top-plate assembly so that it won't bounce around when I start my toenails. I start at one end of the wall, lift up a stud, quickly eyeball it, and lay it back down with the crown pointing to the left (because I'm right-handed). I work my way down the length of the wall until I reach the end (see the photo on the facing page). For 2x6 walls I use 10d commons or 16d sinkers for toenailing. For 2x4 walls I use 8d commons or 10d sinkers. Starting at one end, I start my toenails in the upturned face of each stud—three nails for 2x6, two nails for 2x4. Ideally, the point of the nail should just

peek through the bottom of the stud. I work my way down the row.

Bracing the top plate with my feet, I grab the first stud in my left hand. As I shove it away, I turn it 90° to the right so that it lies on edge, then I pull it back up firmly against the plate. Because the crown now faces up, the stud won't rock on the deck. One blow sets the nail, and two or three more drive it home (see the photo on p. 125). The stud will drift as it's toenailed, depending on the accuracy of the cut, the accuracy of the hammer blow, and the hardness of the wood. Even if you are just a beginning carpenter, you'll quickly learn how far off the mark to start as a way of compensating for the force of your hammer blows.

Crowning and toenailing. Sighting down each stud determines its crown. All the studs are then laid on the top plates with the crowns facing the same direction. The toenails are then started in all the studs and nailed all at once, production-line style.

Through-nailing. As in other methods of framing, the author prescribes through-nailing the bottom of the studs, the jacks, and the cripples. As he works his way down the plate, he aligns each component to its mark and nails it.

Raising the Walls

There are two schools of thought regarding the sequence in which the various walls should be raised. If space on the deck is tight, the long walls must be framed and raised before the other walls have been inflated with studs. Otherwise there won't be enough room. But if I have some room to spare, I'll start with the littlest walls.

I frame the walls and start piling them up. When the pile is finished, the little walls will be on the bottom, and the medium-length walls will be on top. Finally I frame and raise the long exterior walls. Instead of bracing the long walls with a lot of diagonal 2x4s attached to scab blocks, I can pull an adjoining medium-length partition off the pile and drop it into place. This immediately buttresses the long wall. As I work from the perimeter of the house toward the inside, the pile diminishes, and the walls pop up quicker than dandelions.

It may go without saying, but when raising walls, especially long, heavy 2x6 walls, it is important to lift using the power in your legs rather than the smaller muscles in your back. After a wall has been lifted into a vertical position, I ask one person on the crew to line up the bottom plate to the chalkline on the deck while the others hold the wall steady.

The wall can usually be moved to the line by banging on it with a sledgehammer. I nail the bottom plate into the floor framing, one nail per bay. A bay is the space between studs.

All that remains is to rack the walls plumb and brace them. The only braces sticking out into the room should be those necessary to straighten any long, uninterrupted walls that are crooked. The rest of the walls will have been braced by each other. With the next phase of the job already laid out, you're ready to rock and roll.

Scott McBride is a contributing editor to Fine Homebuilding. He is the author of Build Like a Pro: Windows and Doors *(The Taunton Press, Inc., 2002).*

Some carpenters drive a toenail in the 1½-in. edge of the stud to hold it in place, but I've always thought this was a superfluous practice that can be dispensed with. When I reach the end of the wall, I double back, firing nails into the other side of the stud—two nails for a 2x6 stud, one nail for 2x4, staggered with those on the other side.

When the studs, the jacks, and the cripples are toenailed to the top plate, it's time to nail the bottom plate. The bottom plate gets through-nailed to the stud with 16d sinkers—three to a 2x6, two to a 2x4 (see the photo above).

Plumbing, Lining, and Bracing Framed Walls

■ BY SCOT SIMPSON

I have a painting on the wall of my office at home. The painting hangs in a room built in the 1920s or '30s, and the room has 2x4 floor joists and rafters. No matter how hard I try, I can't get the picture to hang straight. My office was probably plumb and straight when it was new, but now it's neither straight nor square nor level. A picture that doesn't hang squarely on a wall might not bug you, but even worse things can go wrong if you build an out-of-square structure.

To avoid these problems, once you've built, stood, and nailed walls together, they must be plumbed and lined. Plumb and line makes walls straight and true. Plumbing is setting a level against the end of a wall to make sure that it stands up straight. Lining is using a tight line attached to the top of a wall to gauge a wall's straightness along its length. You plumb and line walls before installing joists, rafters, and sheathing because it's nearly impossible to move walls after these items are nailed in place.

Doing an inaccurate job will slow down every subsequent framing phase. If exterior

A crowbar provides leverage and control. One person moves the wall; the other tells when the wall is straight up and down, or plumb. Here, a crowbar forces a racking brace forward, moving the top of the adjacent wall. A block nailed to the bottom plate provides even more leverage. When the wall's plumb, the brace is nailed to the bottom plate.

walls aren't straight, you'll have to measure every rafter or floor joist before you cut it; otherwise, it won't fit on the crooked wall. And if you have crooked walls, you'll have bowed siding; you'll have to scribe soffits. You'll have a mess.

If you've framed the floor and the walls carefully, it shouldn't take more than a few hours to plumb and line the walls. You can speed the process by approaching the tasks methodically and by eliminating unnecessary steps.

Start with Careful Layouts and Straight Lumber

When framing walls, you should use the straightest lumber possible for the top and double-top plates, the corner studs, and the end-wall studs. And make sure you cut the bottom and the top plates exactly the same length.

Once walls are stood, be sure all intersecting walls are nailed together tightly and that all double-top plate laps are tight. Intersecting walls must line up in their channels, and corner studs must line up.

Next, bring in your brace lumber—an assortment of 2x4s ranging from 8 ft. to maybe 14 ft., depending on wall height—and distribute the braces throughout the house. These braces help you move walls into position and hold them there until the joists, rafters, and sheathing go on.

To plumb and line, you first get exterior corners standing straight up, or plumb. Next, you straighten the top plates so that they're in line with the walls' corners. Then, you plumb and line any interior walls that intersect exterior walls and finish by plumbing and lining remaining interior walls.

Plumbing Exterior Corners

Pick any exterior corner of the building as your starting point to plumb the walls, but work in one direction after that because when you move one wall, you also move any walls attached to it. Take care not to move walls that you've already plumbed.

You'll need two people—one who will move the wall, the other who will check it for plumb (see the photo on p. 133). The person who's checking the wall puts a level against the end of the wall to see which way it's leaning. I use an 8-ft. level or a 4-ft. level attached to a straightedge that reaches from the top plate to the bottom plate.

A metal fitting lets you work alone. A push stick—a relatively knot-free 10-ft. 2x4—is used to nudge a wall plumb, but it doesn't supply as much leverage as a racking brace and a crowbar. The metal fitting at the bottom of the push stick keeps the brace from slipping.

When let-in braces are required, you can use a push stick to square up the walls (see the photo on the facing page). A push stick is usually just a 2x4 that you place against the face of a stud toward the top of the wall. The bottom of the push stick rests on the floor. I bought a bracket from Rack-R that fastens to the bottom of a push stick and keeps it from kicking out. You lean or even step on the push stick to move the wall into plumb. When the person on the level says right on, the let-in bracing is nailed off, pinning the wall plumb.

Unfortunately, a push stick doesn't produce enough force to move rigid walls. Plus, you still need a brace to hold the wall in place.

Because the walls I frame have sheathing, there's no need for let-in wall braces. But I still have to push walls plumb and hold them there until the sheathing goes on, so I use a racking brace. A racking brace is a 10-ft. or 12-ft. 2x4 placed diagonally on the face of a wall. The high end of the brace points in the direction the wall needs to be pushed.

You nail the brace to the top plate. If you're nailing by hand, you probably will want to start two nails in the end before you lift the racking brace into position. Make sure the brace doesn't stick above the wall in the way of joists or rafters.

The bottom end rests on the floor, and you use a crowbar to shove the brace forward, which pushes the wall. A brace installed at a 45° angle gives the best leverage; a steeper angle tends to push the top plate up.

When the person on the level says the wall is plumb, the brace person drives one nail through the brace into the bottom plate. Then, he releases the crowbar from the brace while the other person checks both ends of the wall for plumb. If both ends are good, then a second nail is put into the bottom plate and one nail is set into a stud in the middle of the brace.

Move to the next corner down the line. Move in one direction until all exterior walls are plumb.

Sometimes, the wall doesn't want to rack with a crowbar, but hitting the double-top plate at the end of the wall with a sledge-hammer tends to loosen it up. Also, you can nail a block behind the crowbar to increase leverage when forcing the racking brace.

Lining Exterior Walls

Now, you've got all exterior corners plumb. Next, straighten the walls. I use two methods to do this. First, I rack any interior walls butting into the exterior walls. When these interior walls are plumb and square, the walls they butt into should be straight. I say "should" because sometimes it just doesn't work that way, and you've got to find the problem and fix it. I'll get to how you fix it a little later.

In places where there are no interior walls to rack and push the exterior walls straight,

Line braces hold walls straight. This gable end is straightened and held straight with 2x4 line braces. Note the line running along the blocking. The top of each brace is nailed to the wall just below the plate. The bottom of each brace is left square so that it can be pushed forward with a crowbar, just like a racking brace. When the wall is straight, the line braces are nailed to cleats. The cleats are spiked to the floor joists, not just to the plywood deck.

I use line braces (see the photo on p. 135) to push or pull the top plate into alignment. A line brace is usually a 2x4 face nailed to a stud just beneath the top plate and spiked to a cleat on the floor or to another wall's bottom plate.

Line braces hold the top of a wall in place like a prop, and they keep the wall straight and stable so that it's safe to walk on as you're nailing off joists. Even if the wall is straight, these braces should be placed every 10 ft. along the wall and at breaks in the top and double-top plates, which are typically weaker points. Make sure the line brace doesn't interfere with wall sheathing. Racking braces and line braces usually stay in place until the roof has been framed and the walls and roof have been sheathed.

Using a Stringline

Some carpenters determine where to straighten a wall by sighting along the top plate the way you'd check a board to see which way it crowns. I don't like to sight the plates because it's not always accurate. Often, the edges of the plate lumber are waned: curved instead of square due to bark or defects. And it's easy to be confused by the many lines in a house's frame, which can cause optical illusions.

For a better look at how straight the top plates are, I run a line from one corner of a wall to another, pulled tightly between nails at each end of the top plate. The line tells me how far in or out the wall is, and by matching the top of the wall with the line, I can straighten the wall.

Commonly, lining is done using blocks. You face-nail a piece of 2x lumber at the top corners of a wall, and then string a line on the outside of the blocks (see the photo above). Then, you slide a 2x4 block along the top plate, checking to see where the block pushes against or pulls away from the line. These are the spots where the plate waves in or out, so you'll need to set a line brace or rack an intersecting wall to straighten the top plate. The purpose of the blocks is to

Blocks make sure the line stays straight. A traditional method of lining is to nail blocks at each corner and to string line across the blocks. Blocks hold line away from the plate. Another block gauges distance between string and plate.

hold the line away from the wall so that the line remains perfectly straight regardless of imperfections in the plates. Without blocks, a crooked plate touching the string somewhere along its length would make the string crooked.

For years I used the blocking method. But I once tried a different method, and I haven't gone back. The line method is the better system. It eliminates the extra steps of putting on and taking off the blocks. It also eliminates the problem of getting an accurate reading if the double-top plates aren't exactly flush. With no blocks, you see the line in relation to the whole wall, not just a protruding edge on the top plate.

To set the line, start a 16d nail in the top of the double plate near the end and edge of the wall (see the top photo on the facing page). Then, bend the nail so that the string will be in line with the edge of the top plate and wall below. Cinch a string to the nail about ½ in. above the plate, extend the string to the other end of the wall, and set another nail. Attach the string, pull tight, and secure. The easiest way to secure the string is by placing it around your finger and twisting it three times (see the bottom photo at right). Then, put the string over the nail. Use one hand to pull the string coming onto the nail while the other hand pulls the end of the string coming off the nail. Once the string is tight, wind the loose end around the nail and tie it off so that the coils trap the loose end.

The key to the line method is that the string is in line with the edge of the wall but is ½ in. above the plate. Hence, no blocks are necessary because imperfections in the plate won't touch the string. And with the plate and string so close to each other, you visually can compare the top plate to the string, and adjust the plate accordingly.

Straightening Exterior Walls

To straighten exterior walls, attach a racking brace to each interior wall that runs into the exterior wall. Rack each interior wall until the lined wall is straight, then nail the brace. If an interior wall runs between two exterior walls, you have to line both exterior walls before racking the interior wall with a racking brace.

For sections of wall that do not have walls running into them, place line braces wherever necessary to hold the wall straight.

If the top of a wall leans into the house, I use a crowbar to shove the bottom of a line brace forward and push the wall out.

If the top of a wall leans away from the house, I first try to pull the wall in line by hand with a line brace. If the wall won't budge, I use a pulling brace (see the photo on p. 138). This brace is pretty much like a line brace, except a pulling brace is installed on the flat instead of on edge, and it draws the top of a wall in instead of pushing it out.

The top end of a pulling brace is nailed under the top plate. The bottom end is trapped under a pair of blocks nailed to the

Using a line without blocks. You can tell if a wall is straight by stringing a tight line from one end of a top plate to another. A nail is bent flush with the outside plane of the wall, and another nail is tacked to the opposite corner.

Tying off a line. To secure the line on the nail, pull the string tight, twist your finger around the string three times, and slip the loop over the nail. Then, just wrap the loose end around the nail.

Pulling braces need to be anchored to the floor. When a top plate has to be pulled in, you need a pulling brace, a 2x4 nailed on the flat under the top plate. A short 2x4 then is used to bow the brace upward, hence pulling in the wall's top plate.

Sources

Rack-R
P. O. Box 974
Novato, CA 94948
(415) 897-7044

---

floor. I usually nail the blocks perpendicular to the brace, with the top block offset from the bottom one so that it holds the brace down. The object is to bow the pulling brace upward—which shortens it and draws the top of the wall in—and the blocks hold the brace down better than if nailed to the floor.

To bow the pulling brace, I nail the bottom of a 4-ft. 2x4 block to the floor, jam the top of the block under the brace, and pull the block tighter and tighter under the pulling brace. If the wall's stubborn, I bash the block under the brace with my hammer. Eventually, the block should bend the brace enough to pull the wall into line; at that point I drive a few nails through the pulling brace into the top of the block, which holds the wall in place.

Walls with long headers are notoriously difficult to line, and sometimes you need

more oomph than you can get from a pulling brace. That's when I break out a come-along.

Making Adjustments

If the walls were built perfectly and the floors were all level, you shouldn't have to make any adjustments to your plumbed and lined walls. However, when you're dealing with lumber that varies in dimensions and often is warped and bowed, and when the plate's end cuts may not be exactly square or the sections of plate are not nailed tightly together or kept tight, it's not unusual that some trimming or stretching becomes necessary to get everything straight and plumb.

The first thing to do when an adjustment is needed is to find the mistake. I check the typical trouble spots. First, I check for a tight fit between intersecting top plates. A gap here usually can be corrected by toenailing a 16d nail up through the top plate of the bywall into the top plate of the intersecting wall.

Then, I check that the top and the bottom plates are the same length. Sometimes there are spaces where plates lap; sometimes the plates are different lengths. If plates aren't the same size, you have to make the top plate longer or shorter.

The wall can be made longer with a few easy steps. Pull the nails where the plates lap. Then, plumb the corner, creating a gap in the top plates of the connecting walls. Nail the end stud of the one wall tight to the connecting stud of the other wall and renail the double plate. You'll have a gap in the top plates at the corner, but the walls will be plumb.

The wall can be shortened by loosening the double plate from the top plate, cutting the top plate shorter with a reciprocating saw and nailing the top plates of the two walls tight. If the double-top plate overhangs the exterior, trim it.

Scot Simpson, a framing contractor in Seattle, Washington, is the author of Framing and Rough Carpentry: Basics for Builders *(R. S. Means Co. Inc.).*

Simple Curved Corners

■ BY SCOTT M. CARPENTER

When my brother told me he wanted to convert his basement into a playroom for his children, I winced. I knew he needed the help of a professional builder and that he assumed I would render that help for the relatively modest payment of lunches and dinners (and the periodic use of his services as a master electrician).

He was looking for ideas, and I had two good ones. My first good idea was to let my brother and his wife clean out the basement. My next good idea had to do with the framing. If this space was to be a playroom, how could we make it more playful and less dangerous? Two words: curved corners.

Considering the Options

Tight-radius curves (2 in. or 3 in.) are easy to make if you use a drywall product called Gypcove (distributed by Pioneer Materials, Inc.), but the larger-radius curves I had in mind for the walls and the window returns

Kid-friendly. Curved corners add comfort and safety to a room for children. Bending plywood creates these corners, which are spackled, taped, skim-coated, and painted exactly like drywall.

required something else. In the past, I framed curved corners with radius-cut plywood top and bottom plates that were ribbed with studs and skinned with two layers of ¼-in. drywall. This drywall was wetted down to make it pliable, yet it still didn't bend smoothly; it pleated and took time to finish.

Although I didn't want to hang around at my brother's longer than necessary, and despite the fact that my brother is, well, a cheapskate, we liked the idea of curved corners. Luckily, a material called bending plywood offered a solution that saved enough on construction time to make it more than worth the extra cost of materials.

Bending Plywood

I discovered bending plywood at my lumberyard, but it's more commonly obtained from suppliers of cabinet-making materials (see the Source sidebar). Several species and thicknesses are available; we chose ⅜-in. three-ply mahogany. It cost me $28 per 4x8 sheet, but that was several years ago, and I

was able to buy directly from a distributor. What makes bending plywood different from standard plywood is that it has only three plies, and the inner ply is much thinner than the outer ones. This makes bending plywood flexible. The thinner middle ply has its grain running perpendicular to the outer layers, which gives the plywood its strength. Some sheets are laminated with the grain running in the 4-ft. direction, others in the 8-ft. direction. The direction of the grain determines the direction the sheet will bend. As an experiment, I bent an 8-ft. sheet in a 6-in. radius. The creaking noise it made warned me to run for cover, but it didn't break.

I calculated that a single sheet would yield two 8-ft.-high corners with a 9-in. radius. We had three corners and four window returns, so we bought two 4x8 sheets (grain oriented in the 8-ft. direction) and one 8x4 sheet (grain oriented in the 4-ft. direction) for window-return corners.

Framing the Curves

We began work on the basement by marking the layout of the walls on the floor. We drew all outside corners square, then we measured 9 in. in from each corner: the radius of each curved corner. When we framed, the straight walls stopped at the 9-in. marks.

The studs at the 9-in. marks were wood 2x4s; the rest were metal studs. I use metal studs in basements partly because the quality of lumber is going downhill, and decent wood studs are hard to get, but mostly I use metal studs because they're easy to work with, especially for furring out block walls. A metal stud wall made of 1⅝-in. studs has many advantages over a wood stud wall, including the fact that it's not affected by basement moisture.

With each wall stopped 9 in. short of the square corner, I felt there should be something in the open corners to wrap the bending plywood around. So I made curved forms. I cut 9-in. radius circles from ¾-in. plywood, quartered the circles, and trimmed the points at 45°. I nailed these curved forms into the open corners like shelves at 16 in. o. c. (see the illustration on the facing page), nailing through the end studs and into the forms.

Getting the Bends

An additional stud was turned sideways and nailed to each end stud, on the straight side of the wall, to serve as a backer for the drywall. Lapping the bending plywood halfway over this backer stud made taping easier. Through trial and error we found that if the butt joint between the bending plywood and the drywall is made 3 in. away from the start of the radius, it is easier to feather the bulge of the tape line into the curve of the corner. Turning the backer stud sideways in the wall gave us room to lap the bending plywood 3 in. onto the wall framing with plenty of space left to fasten the drywall.

We also found it easier to cut the bending plywood after it was installed. By leaving it wide, we could use the extra width for leverage as we bent the plywood around a corner. Our system was to screw one edge of a full sheet to a backer stud, and then my brother bent the plywood around the corner while I screwed it to the curved forms every 2 in. with 1¼-in. drywall screws, and finally to the adjacent stud. Then we marked and cut the bending plywood to width in place with a circular saw and finished the cut with a reciprocating saw. The job became physically more difficult when we were installing the last piece from each full sheet, which was only about 27 in. wide.

Having a moisture content between 6% and 10%, bending plywood takes tape and joint compound just as drywall does. The straight walls were skinned with ½-in. drywall that butts the ⅜-in. bending plywood. We feathered the thickness variance with joint compound, taped the seam, and then skim-coated, or covered the entire corner with a layer of joint compound, to smooth out the bending plywood's rough texture. To check the transition from straight wall to curve, I examined the wall with a halogen lamp, which cruelly reveals imperfections.

Sources

Gypcove
distributed by Pioneer Materials, Inc.
9304 East 39th St. N
Wichita, KS 67226
(316) 636-4343

Curved Wall Corner

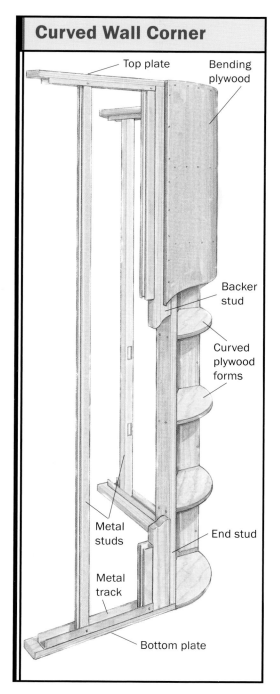

Top plate

Bending plywood

Backer stud

Curved plywood forms

Metal studs

End stud

Metal track

Bottom plate

Brightening the basement. Bending plywood opens up window returns in furred-out walls. The window frame was built up with two layers of conventional plywood, creating pockets that hold the drywall sill and ceiling and the bending plywood returns.

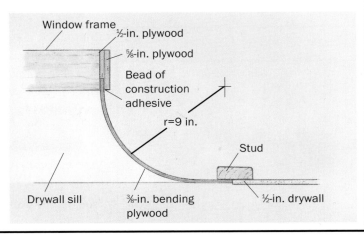

Window frame
½-in. plywood
⅜-in. plywood
Bead of construction adhesive
r=9 in.
Stud
Drywall sill
⅜-in. bending plywood
½-in. drywall

Curved Window Returns

Typically in basement renovations, the exterior walls are furred out to accommodate insulation and electrical wiring, and the windows end up set deep in the wall. We wanted to avoid this look, so we furred out the walls to create 9-in.-radius window returns. These window returns turned out to be successful because they reflect more light into the room than square returns, making the basement brighter.

The fact that my brother decided to replace the old cellar windows with thermopane awning windows, which crank open at the bottom, gave us an opportunity to simplify the window returns. Before mortaring the new windows in place, we built out their frames with two layers of plywood glued on the flat (see the illustration above). The first layer is recessed back from the inside edge of the window frame; the outside layer of plywood is flush with the frame, making a pocket all the way around the window.

After installing the modified windows at the correct height, we slipped the drywall ceiling into the top pocket of each window frame. In the side pockets we squeezed a bead of construction adhesive and inserted bending plywood and screwed it to the wall studs (see the photo above). The tension created by bending the plywood forces it into the pocket and holds it firmly. No other backer or plywood bending forms were required. A drywall sill set into the bottom pocket completed the window return.
Cost estimates are from 1993.

Scott M. Carpenter is a builder in St. Louis Park, Minnesota.

Careful Layout for Perfect Walls

■ BY JOHN SPIER

Framing walls is one of the most fun parts of building a house. It's fast, safe, and easy, and at the end of the day, it's satisfying to admire the progress you've made. Before cranking up your compressor and nailers, though, you need to think through what you're going to do. You need to locate every wall precisely on the subfloor, along with every framing member in those walls.

Layout Starts in the Office

For one of our typical houses, layout and framing for interior and exterior walls start in the office a few days before my crew and I are ready to pick up the first 2x6. First, I review the plans carefully and make sure that all the necessary information is there.

I need the locations and dimensions of all the rough openings, not only for doors and windows but also for things such as fireplaces, medicine cabinets, built-ins, dumbwaiters, and the like. I also make sure the plans have the structural information I need for layout, such as shear-wall and bearing-wall details and column sizes.

At the site, one of Spier's many corollaries to Murphy's Law is that errors never cancel each other out; they always multiply. If the floor is anything but straight, level, flat, and square, the walls are going to go downhill (or uphill) from there. So before you get to layout, do whatever it takes to get a good floor, especially the first: Mud the sills, shim the rims, rip the joists. Sweep off the subflooring, and avoid the temptation to have a pile of material delivered onto it.

Snap Chalklines for the Longest Exterior Walls First

I've learned over the years that it's best to snap the plate lines for the entire floor plan before building any of it. Problems you didn't catch on the prints often jump out when you start snapping lines.

When framing floors, I take great care to set the mudsills flush, square, and in their exact locations. Because the edges of floor framing and subflooring are not always perfect, though, I use a level to plumb up from the mudsills and establish the plate lines, measuring in the stock thickness from the level (see the top left illustration on p. 146). I generally start with the longest exterior walls and the largest rectangle in the plan. When I have the ends of the longest wall located, I snap a line through the marks.

Everything from rafters to kitchen cabinets fits better when you get the walls square and the studs in the right places.

Once I've established the line for the first wall, I move to the parallel wall on the opposite side of the house. I measure across the floor from the first line to the opposite mudsill (again using a level to plumb up from the mudsill to the floor height) at both ends; if the lengths differ slightly, I use the larger measurement. I snap through these points, which gives me two parallel lines representing the long sides of the largest rectangle (see the illustrations at the bottom of p. 146). It's okay if the plates overhang the floor framing by a bit, but I watch for areas that might need to be shimmed or padded—for instance, where a deck ledger needs to be attached to the house.

Establish the Right Angles

I locate three corners by measuring in from the mudsills. The fourth corner I locate by duplicating the measurement between the first and second because I need sides of equal lengths to create a rectangle. I check this rectangle for square by measuring both its diagonals (see the photo at right on p. 146). If I've done everything right so far, the diagonal measurements should be very close, perhaps within ¼ in. I shift two corners slightly if I need to, making sure to keep the lengths of the sides exact until the diagonals are equal. Now, perpendicular lines are snapped through the corners, completing the rectangle.

Because I started arbitrarily with one long wall, I may find now that the rectangle, while being perfectly square, is slightly askew from the foundation and floor. Also, some of the complicated foundations that I work on can have wings or jogs that are slightly off. If I can make everything fit better by rotating the rectangle slightly, I take the time to do it now.

Chalkline tip. To snap chalklines for short walls, hook one end of the line to your boot and stretch the other end out to the mark. Rotating your foot slightly aligns the boot end, and you're ready to snap.

Smaller Rectangles Complete the Wall Layout

With the largest part of the plan established, I lay out and snap whatever bays, wings, and jogs remain for the exterior walls. I use a series of overlapping and adjacent rectangles, which I can square by keeping them parallel to the lines of the original rectangle. I again check the right angles by measuring the diagonals.

Often, the plan calls for an angled component such as a bay. If these components are at 45°, I lay them out from right angles by forming and diagonally bisecting a square. For angles that are not 45°, I either can trust the architect's measurements on the plans, or I can use geometry and a calculator. The latter method is more likely to be accurate.

TIP

When reviewing the plans and laying out walls, watch for elements of the design that need to stay symmetrical and make sure symmetrical elements are aligned at the first layout stage.

For the most precise wall layout, plot a series of rectangles that includes every wall. The larger the rectangle, the more accurate the wall position. Begin with the longest walls, and lay out the largest rectangle using diagonal measurements (photo below). Working off established lines and square corners, work down to the smallest rectangle.

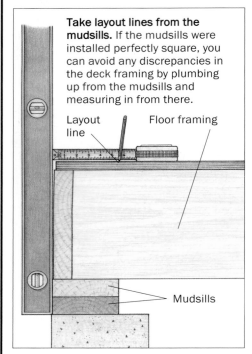

Take layout lines from the mudsills. If the mudsills were installed perfectly square, you can avoid any discrepancies in the deck framing by plumbing up from the mudsills and measuring in from there.

Layout line

Floor framing

Mudsills

Equal diagonal measurements mean a square layout. After snapping chalklines for the longest parallel walls, the author takes corner-to-corner measurements to make sure the corners are square for a perfect rectangle.

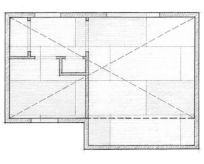

1. **Starting with the longest walls,** measure and square the largest rectangle.

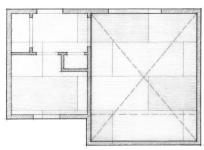

2. **Working off those lines,** plot the rectangle that includes the jog in the wall.

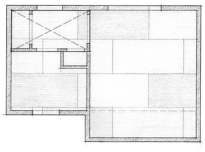

3. **Now measure off the outside** and form a rectangle for the longest interior wall.

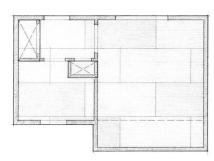

4. **Last, form rectangles** for the remaining interior walls.

Two Quick Layout Tips

Laying Out Multiples

For things such as short closet wall plates, line them up and draw two walls' worth of layout lines at once (photo below left).

Copy the Layout from the Plate

To mark the cripple layout on the rough windowsill, just line it up on the plate and copy the layout (photo below right).

When all the exterior walls have been laid out, I turn my attention to the interior walls. Again, I start with the longest walls and work to the smallest, snapping lines parallel and square to the established lines of the exterior walls. I snap only one side of each plate, but I mark the floor with an X here and there to avoid confusion about where the walls will land. I also write notes on the floor to indicate doors, rooms, fixtures, bearing walls, and other critical information.

It's a rare architect who dimensions a plan to a fraction of an inch with no discrepancies, and an even rarer builder who achieves that accuracy. So first, I lay out critical areas such as hallways, stairwells, chimneys, and tub or shower units, and then I fudge the rest if I need to.

Stud layout is always taken from the same two walls. One crew member holds the tape at wall offset while the other marks the stud position (above). Even when there is a break in the wall, the layout is pulled from the same place to keep all the framing aligned (below).

One last critical issue when reviewing the plans and laying out walls is watching for elements of the design that need to stay symmetrical. If the foundation contractor made one wing a bit wider than another, you don't want to build all three floors before realizing that the ridgelines of the two wings needed to match up. Make sure symmetrical elements are aligned at the first layout stage.

Make Plates from the Straightest Lumber

While I snap the walls, the crew is busy cutting and preparing material from the piles of stock. I have them set aside a pile of the straightest lumber. With the chalklines all snapped and with this material in hand, I start cutting and laying out the plates (top and bottom members) for the exterior walls (see the photo on the facing page). In this step of layout, we set the plates side by side on the layout line, and every wall-framing member is located and labeled. With this

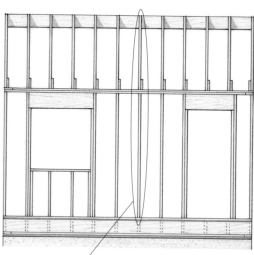

Common layout keeps framing members in line

Pulling the layout from the same point for every level of the house lines up the joists, studs, and rafters for a stronger house that's easier to finish.

Plates on deck. When wall positions are laid out, cut all the top and bottom plates (the long horizontal members) for the exterior walls, and place them on their layout lines.

information, we assemble the walls on the floor, then raise them into place. I often call out measurements and have someone cut and hand up the material to keep mud, snow, and sawdust off the floor during this crucial phase.

As a rule, we plate the longest exterior walls to the corners of the house, and the shorter walls inside them. This approach sometimes needs to be modified—for instance, to accommodate structural columns, hold-down bolts, or openings adjacent to corners. Sometimes an obstruction or a previously raised wall dictates which wall can be built and raised first. The goal here is to build and raise as many walls as possible in their exact positions, especially the heavier ones. Moving walls after they're raised is extra work and no fun.

Before starting any framing, I established a common-stud layout for the entire structure based on two long perpendicular walls from which layout for the rest of the house framing can be measured (see the illustration on the facing page). This common layout keeps joists, studs, cripples, and rafters throughout the house vertically aligned from the foundation to the ridge, which

makes for a strong, straight, and easily finished structure. We use this common layout to locate butt joints between pairs of plates because code and common sense dictate that these joints land on a stud or a header.

As my crew and I measure and cut the pairs of wall plates, we lay them on edge along their layout lines, sometimes tacking them together with just a few 8d nails to keep the plates held together and in place.

Window, Door, and Stud Layout at Last

When all the exterior plates are in place, it's finally time to lay out the actual framing members. I always start with the rough openings for windows and doors. Most plans specify these openings as being a measured distance from the building corner to the center of the opening, which works fine. You can allow for the sheathing thickness or not, but once you choose, be consistent, especially if openings such as windows have to align vertically from floor to floor. Obviously, if an opening such as a bay window or a front door is to be centered on a wall,

Framer's Shorthand: What Those Little Marks Mean

When the framing members are marked, a full-length stud is indicated by an X. A trimmer or jack stud is a T or J, and a C or X indicates a cripple (a short framing member below a sill or above a nonstructural header). Other framing, such as partition posts and corner posts, are labeled along with any special framing instructions.

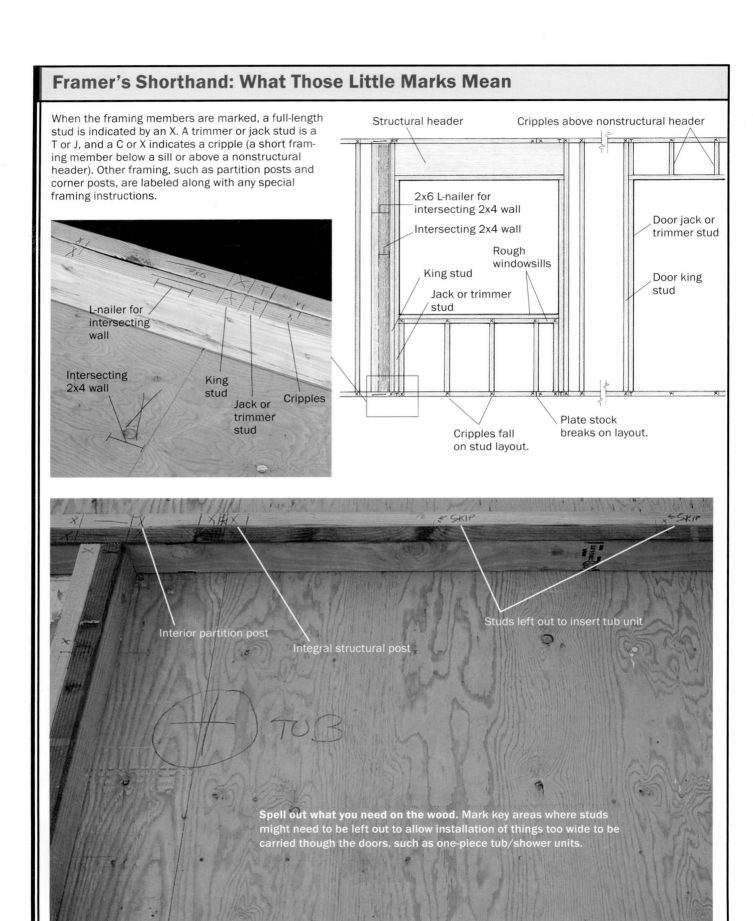

L-nailer for intersecting wall

Intersecting 2x4 wall

King stud

Jack or trimmer stud

Cripples

Structural header

Cripples above nonstructural header

2x6 L-nailer for intersecting 2x4 wall

Intersecting 2x4 wall

Rough windowsills

King stud

Jack or trimmer stud

Door jack or trimmer stud

Door king stud

Cripples fall on stud layout.

Plate stock breaks on layout.

Interior partition post

Integral structural post

Studs left out to insert tub unit

TUB

Spell out what you need on the wood. Mark key areas where studs might need to be left out to allow installation of things too wide to be carried though the doors, such as one-piece tub/shower units.

center it using the actual dimensions of the building, which may differ slightly from the plan.

Rough openings are a subject worthy of their own article, but in a nutshell, I measure half the width of the opening in both directions from the center mark. I then use a triangular square to mark the locations of the edges of trimmers and king studs, still working from the inside of the opening out. Various other marks, such as Xs or Ts, identify the specific members and their positions (see the illustration on the facing page).

Next, I mark where any interior-wall partitions intersect the exterior wall. At this point, I just mark and label the locations; I decide how to frame for them later. I also locate and mark any columns, posts, or nailers that need to go in the wall. I lay out any studs that have to go in specific locations for shelf cleats, brackets, medicine cabinets, shower valves, cabinetry, ductwork, and anything else I can think of. Doing this layout now is much easier than adding or moving studs later.

Finally, I lay out the common studs on the plates. Studs are commonly spaced either 16 in. or 24 in. o. c. to accommodate standard building products. By doing the common-stud layout last, I often can save lumber by using a common stud as part of a partition nailer. I almost never skip a stud because it's close to another framing member, which, I've learned the hard way, almost always causes more work than it saves. I occasionally shift stud or nailer locations to eliminate small gaps and unnecessary pieces. I keep the plywood layout in mind here, though, so that I can use full sheets of sheathing as much as possible.

Inside Walls Go More Quickly

Once the exterior walls are built and standing, I cut the interior-wall plates and set them in place. Where two walls meet, I decide which one will run long to form the corner so that the walls can be built and raised without being moved. Also, facing a corner in a particular direction often provides better backing for interior finishes, such as handrails or cabinetry, and sometimes is necessary to accommodate such things as doorways or multiple-gang switches.

When the plates are cut and set in place, I do the stud layout. Just as with the exterior walls, I do the openings first, then nailers and specific stud and column locations. Next, I mark the locations of intersecting walls and finally overlay the common-stud layout on the plates.

Where Walls Come Together

Where one wall meets the middle of another, I use a partition post if the situation dictates it, but more often, I opt for an L-nailer. To make an L-nailer, I use a wider stud on the flat next to a common stud whenever possible. It's faster and easier; it accommodates more insulation; and it saves the subs from drilling through those extra studs and nails. If I use U-shaped partition posts (a stud or blocks on the flat flanked by two other studs) in an exterior wall, I need to make sure to fill the void created by the partition post with insulation before the sheathing goes on.

With the interior plates all there, we can nail in the studs, raising walls as we go. I mark key areas where studs should be crowned or specially selected, such as areas with long runs of cabinetry, and also studs that might need to be left out to allow installation of things too wide to be carried though the doors. I also nail double top plates to as many walls as possible if they don't interfere with the lifting process.

John Spier and his wife, Kerri, own Spier Construction, a custom building company on Block Island, Rhode Island.

CREDITS

INDEX

Taunton's FOR PROS BY PROS Series

A collection of the best articles from *Fine Homebuilding* magazine.

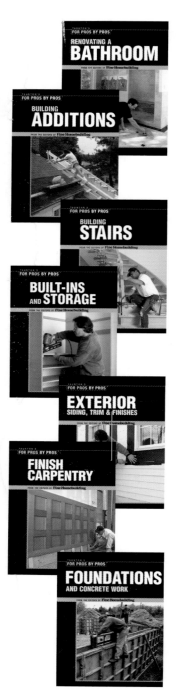

Other Books in the Series:

Taunton's For Pros By Pros:
RENOVATING A BATHROOM

ISBN 1-56158-584-X
Product #070702
$17.95 U.S.
$25.95 Canada

Taunton's For Pros By Pros:
BUILDING ADDITIONS

ISBN 1-56158-699-4
Product #070779
$17.95 U.S.
$25.95 Canada

Taunton's For Pros By Pros:
BUILDING STAIRS

ISBN 1-56158-653-6
Product #070742
$17.95 U.S.
$25.95 Canada

Taunton's For Pros By Pros:
BUILT-INS AND STORAGE

ISBN 1-56158-700-1
Product #070780
$17.95 U.S.
$25.95 Canada

Taunton's For Pros By Pros:
EXTERIOR SIDING,
TRIM & FINISHES

ISBN 1-56158-652-8
Product #070741
$17.95 U.S.
$25.95 Canada

Taunton's For Pros By Pros:
FINISH CARPENTRY

ISBN 1-56158-536-X
Product #070633
$17.95 U.S.
$25.95 Canada

Taunton's For Pros By Pros:
FOUNDATIONS AND
CONCRETE WORK

ISBN 1-56158-537-8
Product #070635
$17.95 U.S.
$25.95 Canada

Taunton's For Pros By Pros:
RENOVATING A KITCHEN

ISBN 1-56158-540-8
Product #070637
$17.95 U.S.
$25.95 Canada

Taunton's For Pros By Pros:
FRAMING ROOFS

ISBN 1-56158-538-6
Product #070634
$17.95 U.S.
$25.95 Canada

Taunton's For Pros By Pros:
BUILDING PORCHES AND
DECKS

ISBN 1-56158-539-4
Product #070636
$17.95 U.S.
$25.95 Canada

Taunton's For Pros By Pros:
BUILDING TIPS AND
TECHNIQUES

ISBN 1-56158-687-0
Product #070766
$17.95 U.S.
$25.95 Canada

Taunton's For Pros By Pros:
ATTICS, DORMERS, AND
SKYLIGHTS

ISBN 1-56158-779-6
Product #070834
$17.95 U.S.
$25.95 Canada

For more information visit our website at www.taunton.com.